A Local Boy Goes to War

Memories of World War II

By Lawrence P. Titzler

Cazenovia Books

Buffalo (USA)

Published by Cazenovia Books, Buffalo, New York

Printed in the United States of America

ISBN-13: 978-1717597687

First Edition

In Honor of

Irene Titzler

July 12, 1925 - May 09, 2014

War is never over
Though the treaties may be signed
The memories of the battles
Are forever in our minds

War is never over
So when you welcome heroes home
Remember in their minds they hold
Memories known to them alone

— Cecil L. Harrison

CONTENTS

Acknowledgements

So many people contributed to make this publication possible and I hope I do not leave anyone out.

From my war years, I want to thank my Company Commander, Captain Andrew C. Heath (KIA), who led us through the Battle of the Bulge; and his successor, Captain Randolph Linhart, who was Company Commander during operations at the Remagen Bridge. My mentor and counsel throughout the war was Staff Sergeant Robert Strusa, a Medical Technician.

Many people helped with the book project itself. Ema Makas worked diligently and faithfully for two years on her computer to edit my handwritten notes. She did extensive editing and corrections. Without her persistence, invaluable expertise and computer skills, this book would never have been published.

Joseph Elliott, grandson of Robert Strusa, served as my volunteer Military Research Editor and this book would not have been published without his invaluable assistance. He engaged in exhaustive research about his grandfather's and my military career and awards.

My beloved parents, Elizabeth and Peter Titzler, endured the war years with unrelenting worry and concern and prayer.

My dear friends Peter and Ellen Reese carefully reviewed and greatly improved the manuscript.

Anna Karin Ostrowski served ably as my editor at Cazenovia Books. Suzanne M. Pulk did a marvelous job with the cover.

Finally, I wish to thank Congressman Brian Higgins (NY-26) and Supervisor Anthony Caruana who presented me with the Bronze Star and other medals I earned for my service in the United States Army during World War II. My county legislator Kevin Hardwick was also of great assistance in that process. As part of his research, Mr. Elliott

Acknowledgements

contacted Congressman Higgins' office on my behalf. Thanks to the combined efforts of these men, I was presented in 2014 with the Bronze Star Medal, the Combat Medical Badge 1st Award, Good Conduct Medal, Meritorious Unit Commendation, American Campaign Medal, European-African-Middle Eastern Campaign Medal with 2 bronze service stars, World War II Victory Medal, Army of Occupation Medal with Germany Clasp and the Honorable Service Lapel Button--World War II.

As I appraise my 95 years of life, I must acknowledge the love and devotion for my family that will remain with me into eternity. My wife Irene, who went to God on May 9, 2014, was married to me for over 63 years. Our love was complete and everlasting. Endearing memories of our children complement our marriage. Our daughter Susan (husband Chris) was always loving and caring and has a successful career as a senior entertainment reporter for *USA Today*. My son Paul (wife Deb) has a successful career in human relations.

My grandson, David (wife Becca), is a computer engineering manager for IBM. He and his wife have made me proud to be a great grandfather to Emma, Ben and Jacob Lawrence who was born this year. My second grandson, Jeffrey, is an honorably discharged Iraq War veteran where he served as a paratrooper.

My cup runneth over!

Lawrence P. Titzler
Tonawanda, New York
June 2018

Prologue

This book is not intended to be a historical and factual presentation of WWII. Now, as a senior citizen, 70 plus years after the conclusion of the war, I have frequently reflected upon my entire life, which began shortly before the beginning of the Great Depression (in the 1930s) and is continuing.

My simple, naïve, shy and restricted life was interrupted on Pearl Harbor Day in 1941. My entire life was torn apart, and my complex, more dangerous and rapidly maturing life had now begun.

The tragic and humorous events that have occurred to me throughout my lifetime remain immensely vivid in my mind. These chapters are a detailed description of my journey up until my Army discharge in 1946. The book may conclude here, but my adult life continued with my college education, provided by the G.I. Bill of Rights, my wonderful marriage (63½ years) to my wife, Irene, the birth of my two children, Susan and Paul, my grandchildren David (wife Rebecca), and Jeffrey, my great-grandchildren, Emma, Ben and Jacob Lawrence and my successful career in public school education as a teacher and administrator.

1.   My Memorable Pre-War Childhood

As I move through the routines of daily life, feasting on a simple breakfast in my kitchen, I begin to notice the arrival of winter upon my windowsill. Another season of my life, another stepping-stone to mark my journey. Universally speaking, I have rotated around the sun 95 times (380 seasons), thus far . . .

In the midst of my casual state, I begin to reflect upon my life and contemplate its underlying significance. I am well aware that my life is not the peak of God's creation, rather a blip, a flickering beam of light within his wondrous universe. Each life is a contributing component, and every life carries a message, forever leaving an imprint on the universe. Life is an all-inclusive mixture of everything, including nothingness. It is an amalgamation of passion, love, hatred, sorrow, and fear. My message has always centered upon my gratefulness towards God, and my contribution to my friends, relatives, associates, caregivers, neighbors . . . and country.

As 2018 begins, I deeply mourn the passing of my true love, my wife of 63 years, 5 months, and 16 days, Irene. Irene and I met on February 7, 1946, and we married, for better or for worse, on November 23, 1950 (Thanksgiving Day). She died in my arms on May 9, 2014.

Perhaps because of loneliness and the need for more socialization, my thoughts have centered upon my life's contributions to my family, friends and country. My reflections have become more vivid and not so distant.

I was born on January 31, 1923, in my parents' rented home on Esser Avenue, in the Riverside area in North Buffalo. A successful delivery was accomplished in an Esser Avenue bedroom, by Anna

My Memorable Pre-War Childhood

Eichorn, an immensely experienced midwife, and family friend. I entered the post-World War I era when I was introduced to my parents Elizabeth and Peter, who were 1912 immigrants from the *Banat* area of central Europe. In addition, I was introduced to my older brother, Frank, who was born on May 30, 1914.

In 1926, my parents had a home built at 128 Condon Avenue in the Riverside area near Esser. Within the vicinity of my home, I had Riverside Park, Murtagh's candy store and ice cream parlor, Riverside Theater, Rowland's Department store (toy department), the Riverside Men's Shop, and a Buffalo Public Library Branch; all these locations were within a half of mile from our home. These were the years (1926-1942) of my preteen and teenage era that forever remain vivid and memorable to me.

While my family and I still resided on Esser Avenue, I had a nanny named Mrs. Becker, who lived next door. We referred to her as *Becker Nanny*, and she was my nanny for approximately two years. One day, I recall my mother holding me in her arms, looking out our large dining room window. We were facing Becker Nanny's window, and Becker Nanny herself. Becker Nanny had a cloth dust mop on a pole in her hand, and I remember her waving to me with that mop. My first instinct was to think of it as a monster. I remember the strands of fabric eerily swaying back and forth, taunting me. It frightened me immensely to say the least, and I still *vividly* remember that *mop scare* to this day.

When I reached the mature age of five, my parents naturally wanted to put me into school. One would never guess, especially because of how fluent my English has turned out, but as a five-year-old child of German-speaking immigrants I could not speak English, and therefore could not be accepted into school (Kindergarten, School 65). After one year of home teaching by my mother (to learn the English language), I was accepted into Public School 65 at the Kindergarten level. I surprised the teacher because I even knew the alphabet.

I was 6 years old when the Great Depression began. It was October, 1929. Following the decade of the 1920's, when economic conditions were very high and illegal alcohol establishments were immensely prominent, the stock market and Wall Street experienced a historical fall which resulted in huge unemployment statistics, breadlines, and suicides. During the Great Depression, approximately 15 million Americans were out of work. Jobs were scarce, pay was minimal, and the economy was unbelievably poor. I remember my parents one day quietly conversing, (trying to be as discreet as possible, so that I could not hear or understand them), discussing how to pay the mortgage and other household bills. Prices were extremely low then (in comparison to prices today), but then again, so was the family income.

My parents regularly enjoyed a fish fry at a place around the corner, *Scoop's Restaurant*. The fish fry cost $1.00, including a soft drink. I went along many times and enjoyed the meal and soft drink, for a child's price of 50 cents. Such prices are unbelievable for this present-day, it certainly almost seems like a different world.

My father was a self-employed barber. He was not especially wealthy but was considered wealthy by neighbors when he was earning about $20 per week. He owned his own barber shop on Tonawanda Street in the Riverside area. It was across from Riverside Park, and it meant a lot to me because it is where I spent most of my hours throughout my pre-teen years, enjoying the playgrounds, swimming pool areas, and the ice cream soda store right next to my father's barber shop. Mr. Murtagh, the owner of the ice cream store, was a friend of my father, and I would occasionally receive a *free* chocolate ice cream cone.

Before my parents met in Buffalo, my mother was a nanny and housekeeper for a well-to-do family, in Atlanta, Georgia. As mentioned before, I did not grow up in an immensely privileged family or under extravagant circumstances. We were not poor, nor extremely wealthy.

I recall the summer of 1928 when I was hurt in an auto accident. The Deli on the corner of Esser and Condon (Hohl's Deli) sold candy suckers on a stick *with* a ring for a penny. My mother gave me a penny and warned me to cross the Esser/Condon intersection carefully. I was so overly anxious to get my ring and candy that I ended up not being as careful as I should have been while crossing.

My Memorable Pre-War Childhood

Before I knew it, I was struck by a speeding car. The accident resulted in a broken collarbone and an epidemic of bruises. I also had to wear a dreadful upper back brace for *two whole months*, *and*, I had to postpone my attendance to the first grade for *half of the year*. This lesson surely taught me that parents sometimes do seem overprotective *with reason*.

In 1933, my father purchased a German Shepherd dog named Tessie. From then on, I had a protector. My parents kept him in the garage to serve as a guard dog, protecting maintenance and yard equipment. He was an immensely faithful dog that snarled and barked loudly. Moreover, thanks to him, no one ever dared to remove any equipment from the garage. We greatly appreciated him for that. I frequently worried my mother because I always wanted to open the garage door to go in to hug and pet him. He loved my companionship, and I know that because he licked me all the time. He protected me. No one ever tried to shout or hit me, or else he would snarl, bite, or attack. He was my first dog and I will always remember him. It is surreal, the bond that can occur between a man and his dog.

In later life I had two other dogs – a Dachshund (Rudy) and a Beagle (Sunshine), but Tessie was always first with me, until my fourth dog, T.R., a West Highland Terrier, who also held a very special place in my heart. He arrived into my life in the year 2012, when he was five years old, as an adopted dog from the local SPCA.

T.R. was a very faithful, gentle and loving animal; but he had to be put down because of extensive tumors and cancer. He was put to sleep as I was holding him in my arms. The veterinarian knew that this was an extremely traumatic experience for me, and she allowed me to keep him in my arms for an additional twenty minutes. Since my love for dogs was so great, the SPCA found another dog for me. My new and present dog is a Maltese Poodle named Buddy; an energetic and loving puppy.

Now to recall memories of another immensely important individual and influence throughout my life: my grandfather. His name was Lawrence; "coincidentally" we have the same name. His wife, my grandmother, was named Katherine. To this day, I remember sharing a bed with him as he told me simply fascinating stories of his youth and native country. He died in the year 1933, when I was only ten years old. Even though I was rather young, I still remember him and our times together. He was a great man and he had the power to tell stories that could take you to another dimension.

His wake and casket were on the first floor of our Condon Avenue home, just below my bedroom on the 2nd floor. I was beyond frightened and nervous, but to get through I remembered his stories. I especially clung to the knowledge that every time the thunder roared, it was him bowling in heaven. This reassured me and still does to this day. It is remarkable that such a small and seemingly insignificant story could have such a lasting and positive influence on you forever.

Another important figure in my life was my older brother, Frank. He was a chain smoker since the age of 8. Cigarettes were very cheap at that time, approximately 15 cents (per package) or so. Regardless, Frank could not afford to buy them regularly, so he rolled his own cigarettes with a roller mechanism and recruited me to roll them for him. You could say that this was a form of bonding between the two of us. Incidentally, I had never smoked at the time and never would in the future. Due to the nine-year age difference, my brother and I were not as close as I would have preferred. When I was ten, he was nineteen. He had teenage friends interested in fishing, boating, and hunting, while I was always studious, a complete bookworm, who enjoyed listening to radio stories. In his later life, my brother married my sister-in-law, Ann, moved to the West Coast, and became the father of eight children.

I loved listening to *The Shadow,* a detective mystery show, and *Jack Armstrong* (the All-American Boy), another detective mystery about a high school amateur detective and athlete. In addition, I loved watching the double feature of *Mickey Mouse* at the movie theater every Saturday. My *favorite* routine on the weekends was listening to "Hit Parade," the top ten songs for the week. This was on every Saturday evening at 9 pm. George Gershwin, Cole Porter, and Jerome Kern, were three very popular composers at the time. In addition, from Monday to Friday, I listened to 15-minute soap operas. My favorites were *Myrt and Marge* (mother and daughter) and *Just Plain Bill* (wise father). Radio shows were immensely memorable to me. I happened to be listening to *The Shadow* (at 5 p.m.) when the historic Pearl Harbor announcement of the Japanese attack was made on December 7, 1941.

As for movies, I will never forget the original *King Kong*. It was an immensely popular and unique movie at the time. I saw it with my cousin, in 1933, in Chicago, when I was only ten years old. Seeing the movie at such an early age made it seem *much* scarier; this is part of why I have never forgotten the experience. To this day, I recall our excitement and our act of pretending that we were more mature than we actually were. This was a memorable day for me.

When I was about 13 years of age, my mother wanted me to take piano lessons. She paid for a teacher to come once a week and give me hour-long lessons. I disliked this a great deal because I always felt that I had no talent. From time to time, my mother would ask me to play piano to entertain her friends, and this was *immensely* embarrassing for me. The music that I did enjoy (with my lack of talent) included "Blue Danube" (Beautiful) and "Whistle While You Work" from Snow White. I still enjoy those songs to this day.

My years as a student greatly shaped me as a person. From first grade to third grade, I attended the All Saints School on Esser Avenue. This school was rather strict, as we were disciplined by nuns. Later, I was enrolled at P.S. #60 on Ontario Street, in the Riverside area of Buffalo for grades four through eight. While there, I learned to become a rather impressive speller. I even won the classroom spelling bee in 7th grade. As a result of winning the classroom bee, I was qualified to be in the school spelling bee, with a larger range of students.

On the day of the school spelling bee, Mr. Cobb, the principal, arranged the seating and order on the stage. I was in the first row, second seat. After a fair amount of anticipation, the spelling bee commenced, and the first finalist proceeded to stand in center of attention. Mr. Cobb gave him a word to spell; he spelled the word correctly, with ease, and afterwards he simply sat back down in his seat.

My turn was next. I stood up and Mr. Cobb asked me to spell the word *ability*. You could say that I was experiencing a bit of stage fright. I looked into the crowd and saw a pool of parents and students. This made me remarkably nervous, and in my defense, this was my first experience in a spelling bee of such grand scale. I eventually proceeded to spell the given word (ability). I managed to get through the first two letters (A-B), but after that, my mind hit repeat and simply went blank. I repeated "A-B, A-B, A-B" *at least* a dozen times. What eventually put my "A-B's" to a halt was a booming voice from the audience that shouted "AB, please answer him so that he will stop calling for you!" Laughter erupted throughout the room. I cannot put into words how much this humiliated me.

Mr. Cobb, after being ever so patient with me, politely asked me to sit back down. I sat there, first row, second seat, until the end of the bee. I decided right then and there, no future spelling bees for me. I was done with my spelling bee career. Although, I will admit, that to this day, I still consider myself an impressive speller.

I attended Riverside High School from 1936-1940. It is true to say that I was an introvert, very shy, and kept to myself. The 1940 yearbook motto under my picture was; "Larry knows that speech is silver but believes in silence golden." I would say, this, in short speech, summarizes my personality rather accurately.

I needed some close friends in my senior year, so I formed a group called "The Skull Club," with Billy Anderson and Victor Group. We would alternate the "club meetings" among our three houses and we even had "club sweaters" with black and white skulls on them. One of the *exciting* things that we did was sell candy. With this money we were able to raise the funds needed for a week-long summer trip to Allegany State Park where we rented a cabin in the Quaker Run area in 1940. A cabin rental for a week cost approximately ten dollars. Our transportation was my 1930 Model A Ford, with a rumble seat. My brother donated it to me after buying himself a new car. Allegany is an immensely memorable vacation spot for me. Although, it would probably have been a little better if I wasn't selected as our cook while there. I genuinely had no idea how to prepare food. My *specialty* was spaghetti. Thankfully, Mrs. Anderson (Billy's mom) cooked for us on the last day; providing a phenomenal last meal to top off our trip.

Despite my poor cooking, we had the time of our lives during our week at the State Park. A group of five teenage girls from Jamestown, New York rented the cabin next door. *Innocence* was the descriptive word to describe our week together.

Billy Anderson was my best friend. After our childhood and teenage years, he served in World War II as a tail gunner over Germany (1943-1945). Billy and Victor drifted apart after high school, whereas Billy and I always kept in touch here and there throughout our lives. I even went to his funeral a few years ago. To this day he is certainly someone that I *will not* and simply *cannot* ever forget. Billy Anderson was truly a friend for life. I salute him for his bravery and his service in the U.S. Army Air Corps.

To be quite honest, I never really traveled much outside of my small world. The trip to Allegany was one exception (although not far from home), and then the other exception would be the train ride that I took to Chicago in 1933 to visit my mother's side of the family. My mother and her sister at the time attended the *World's Fair* in Chicago. I was not allowed to go, but either way, I was excited to be out of my ordinary element and experiencing Chicago in any way possible.

Unfortunately, the train ride was very uncomfortable and seemed to go on forever. However, I was impressed by the duties of the conductor and the porter serving beverages.

For as long as I can remember, I have been nearsighted. My mother and I never accepted this even though throughout my school years, I struggled to see the chalkboard. To counteract this handicap, I always asked for a front row seat in any classroom, as close to the chalkboard as possible. Even then, I could not see everything clearly. Sometimes I would even stay after class and copy everything that the teacher put on the board. I was consistently a good student. I must credit this effort, my diligence, hard work, and good memory, because I have always been on the honor roll. Upon induction into the U.S. Army, the army medical team immediately discovered my poor eyesight and brought it to my attention. The U.S. Army gave me the option of refusing my induction and accepting a 4F deferment; but instead, I chose to spend three years in the U.S. Army, which was the best decision of my young life. To date, I am extremely proud of my decision to accept Army induction and to have made my small contribution in gaining our WWII victory. My mother did not know and never did learn that I had the option to refuse Army induction.

When I put my first army-issued glasses on, it seemed like a miracle, and all around me seemed like a whole new world. Everything was so clear and distinct that it also made me feel like a *new person*, reborn. Since that date, in 1943, I have always worn glasses. I have never regretted my choice to remain in the military service and as I look back at everything, over 70 plus years, I know that the Lord was looking after me, keeping me out of harm's way, and setting my future to one of contentment and happiness with no regrets. With time this became more and more apparent to me; especially after falling in love with my beautiful wife, Irene, marrying her on November 23, 1950, becoming a father and watching my children, Paul and Susan, grow. I made unforgettable friends, and had a remarkable career in education, as a public-school teacher and administrator. Paul received a BS degree in Business Administration from Canisius College and Susan received a BA degree in English from Canisius College along with a Master's Degree in Journalism from Syracuse University. Paul's education resulted in a lifetime career as a Human Resource Director, while Susan became the senior entertainment reporter for the USA Today newspaper.

2.   Attack on Pearl Harbor

I graduated from Riverside High School in June 1940. It marked the beginning of a brand-new phase in my life, the beginning of my leap into adulthood. After high school, I attended Chown School of Business (from September 1940 to June 1941). There, I met Dr. Lewis Bates Clark. He was my memorable accounting professor and an immense inspiration. His advice sparked my interest to study becoming a CPA later in my life.

Shortly after attending the Chown School of Business, I found my first job. I began working at Great Lakes Engineering, located on Woodward Avenue in the Town of Tonawanda. I was hired as a payroll accountant, working full-time, 40 hours per week. I was earning a weekly paycheck of approximately 18 dollars. Nowadays, 18 dollars seems more fitting to be an hourly wage, rather than a sum for a weekly paycheck. I have mentioned before, it is quite astonishing to ponder over how the economy and financial values have changed throughout the years.

The majority of employees at Great Lakes Engineering worked in the large machine shop. Every shift, they would punch their personal time cards, which showed their starting and ending labor times. These employees were paid between 55 to 75 cents per hour, depending on their experience. The machine shop supervisor was paid approximately 88 cents per hour; this was considered an exceptionally high salary.

Ultimately, my job was to review the time cards and record the exact hours worked by every employee. With this information, including hourly pay rate and taxes, I would then calculate their weekly salaries. Since this was my first job, I certainly did not want to disappoint. I would certainly say that I did immensely well here; I worked here for over a year (from July 1941 to December 1942), up until receiving my so-called "greeting from Uncle Sam" in late December 1942.

December 7, 1941, Pearl Harbor Day, was the conclusion of my childhood. It was the end of my comfortable lifestyle of 18 years; living a humble life in the Riverside area of Buffalo. My routine walks to the Riverside Theatre every Saturday and Sunday (at 1:00 p.m.) were coming to a conclusion.

Matinee admission was 15 cents, and an extra five cents for a bag of popcorn or a large candy bar. The matinee included Movietone World News, a Disney cartoon, an episode of a 12-chapter dramatic serial (with suspenseful endings, to anticipate for next week), and two feature full length movies of high quality. You could remain for the second showing, starting at about 5:00 p.m., for no extra cost. Movietone World News concentrated primarily on the Pearl Harbor attack and the beginning of America's war actions against Japan and Germany. This was the most popular and relevant news. As I previously mentioned, the first radio announcement regarding Pearl Harbor occurred while I was absorbed in listening to my radio serials. These programs were gradually eliminated when the war began, because then all networks turned their attention to war programs and heroism.

On December 8, 1941, President Franklin Delano Roosevelt stood before Congress and requested a declaration of war against Japan. His statement to Congress was; "Yesterday, December 7, 1941—a date which will live in infamy—the United States of America was suddenly and deliberately attacked by naval and air forces of the Empire of Japan."

In December 1942, at the age of 19 (soon to be 20), I received what was called a "greeting from the federal government." It was a notice to report to my army draft officer in Riverside for probable induction into the U.S. Army. Induction required passing a thorough physical exam, in the downtown post office building in Buffalo (now the Erie Community College building). The following week, I reported for the physical exam. I passed everything, except for my eye exam; as mentioned before, growing up I had always struggled with my eyesight. My draft board did not fail me but gave me the choice of being drafted or granted a 4F (incapable of Army service). The memory of the many Americans who died at Pearl Harbor and my strong patriotic feelings were the primary factors that made me decide to accept enlistment. I wanted to do something *for* my country. I never told my parents that I had made this decision, in spite of my eyesight problem.

3.   A New World and New Life

I was inducted into the United States Army on January 23, 1943. I pledged allegiance to my country and to the United States and was officially inducted before the draft board members in the Riverside Draft Board Office. This was one of the proudest moments of my life.

At 4:00 p.m. on January 23, 1943, after approval by the local draft board in North Buffalo (Riverside), I boarded a school bus at the corner of Ontario and Tonawanda Street. I was accompanied by 32 other inductees; and we began our *long* journey of about 30 miles. We passed Niagara Falls and Lewiston, NY, all the way to Youngstown, NY, the location of Fort Niagara; the primary induction center in western New York. Since I was a completely inexperienced traveler, this trip of

The Author at Fort Niagara

30 miles seemed endless to me, I would have easily believed that it was a 500-mile trip. The other inductees seemed to be very much at

ease and were singing "We're in the Army Now." I should have been singing "Home Sweet Home."

Upon arrival at the outer gates of the Fort, the slightly intimidating military policemen (MP), boarded our bus with pistols at their sides to check for any unusual conditions or materials. While they were leaving the bus, one MP commented that our group looked like a bunch of kids, but was sure that we would leave as dedicated and honored G.I.'s.

We entered the Fort and drove straight ahead past acres of fields on which were erected one-story, long wooden barracks. The barracks had originally been erected about five to seven years earlier to be used as billets for young unemployed men who joined the Civil Conservation Corp (CCC). The CCC was formed by the federal government during the Great Depression to create jobs in Niagara County and to aid in conservation and general improvement of undeveloped acres of land in northern Niagara County. Unknown to me at the time, those barracks would be our "residence" starting later that day.

We went about another half mile down the road and arrived at a brick, three-story, steam-heated building. We were told to exit the bus and line up in a long, single row on the first floor. It was time for me

The Glamorous Barracks at Fort Niagara

to experience the most humiliating experience of my 19 years of life.

A very rough, strong-voiced first-sergeant shouted and commanded that the 30+ recruits "immediately drop their pants and underwear." After a few more loud commands, all my fellow recruits did as told, except for me. The sergeant came face to face with me and said, "Drop them now or I'll take them off for you! This means underwear too!" I was mortified; and with great hesitation, I finally followed orders, still not exactly knowing why this was necessary.

An Army officer appeared wearing a white medical coat. He announced that this was a required venereal disease inspection. He put on white sterile gloves and began with the first recruit. He handled the penis of each man and squeezed to see if any tell-tale white and bloody liquid would appear. I cannot put into words how awkward the entire process was; but thankfully, all the new recruits ended up passing the extremely uncomfortable and invasive exam. The officer (a doctor) made it a point to talk to me and said, "I thought you would faint, but you survived, and you have had no sexual contact thus far in your life. You will have a good career in the Army!" I was relieved to receive *some* words of encouragement after such a humiliating scene.

I noticed that some previous inductees were residing on other floors of this brick, steam-heated building, and naively, I thought that we would join them.

Unfortunately, we were put back on the bus and taken to the unheated Civilian Conservation Corps (CCC), one-story wooden buildings. My first shock was the venereal disease inspection; my second was the mere sight of my army cot and the single blanket that would be my companion for my two-week stay at Fort Niagara.

Each recruit was assigned the task of feeding logs into the old pot-bellied stove that served as the sole source of heat in the barracks. I was assigned to the midnight to 2:00 a.m. shift. I had no idea or experience about when to add wood or how to stoke the fire to prevent it from extinguishing. Needless to say, I was not very successful at my task and was always very grateful when my 2:00 a.m. replacement arrived to restore the flames and heat.

Reveille sounded at 4:30 a.m. every morning, giving us only 15 minutes to dress into our crisp, new army uniforms. We were then expected to line up outside the barracks for inspection by the officer in charge. After passing his inspection, we were issued a *mess-kit*, and then with it we went to the next building where what they referred to

19

as "breakfast" was slapped into our kits. Another surprise? I think not.

After several weeks at Fort Niagara, I realized that I was the only inductee from my group that had not been assigned to another Army division or destination. I was kept at Fort Niagara to explain and clarify the availability of veterans' life insurance. This was my temporary assignment when I was not required to take numerous aptitude and IQ tests that might give clues to indicate where I could be of most benefit in the military service.

4.   Outstanding Education Provided

After two short assignments at Pine Camp, N.Y. (now Fort Drum), and Plattsburgh, NY, (and after completing more tests); I was accepted into the ASTP program at Princeton University on March 1, 1943. A U.S. Army assignment to an Army Specialized Training Program at Princeton University (or any other American University) is comparable to West Point; strict rules and regulations had to be followed or else dismissal from the program would promptly be made. Poor grades would also call for dismissal. The scores of

U. S. O., Plattsburg, New York

my Army aptitude and intelligence tests were high and were the primary reason for my acceptance into the ASTP Engineering program. I had a tremendous disadvantage in my advanced math and science classes because of my non-college oriented high school program. My lower grades in math and chemistry caused me great concern; although, I received educational aid from my fellow new-found Army friend and dormitory roommate, Norman Garvelmann. He was from the Bronx, New York and overall a very nice guy; moreover, he was familiar with Princeton's math programs and he spent a great deal of effort trying to update my knowledge. With his help, along with applying a bit of common sense on the multiple-choice tests (which were the basis of grades received), I was able to continue at the ASTP.

My successful grade of "A" in geology was due to my long interest in the land, weather, oceans, and general composition of this

Princeton University

planet; *and* my good relationship with my geology professor's daughter. I met her at their home when I came to meet her for a Sunday walk around Lake Carnegie, adjoining the campus. Lake Carnegie was known for rowing competitions against Yale, Harvard, Dartmouth, and other colleges. I must say that a Sunday afternoon walk around the lake, on a pleasant stone walkway, surrounded by a plethora of weeping willows and well-groomed grass, was truly the definition of bliss.

My Sunday date encouraged me to spend time sitting on the grass, under the secluded trees;

after a while, she decided that this was a rather romantic atmosphere and decided to get comfortable in a prone position, while asking me to join her. I was aware of what the result might be and that this would probably be observed by the Sunday walkers. My body was ready to cooperate, but my brain kept warning me that such activity, involving a faculty member's family, could potentially get me dismissed from Princeton. It was not a risk that I was willing to take. My brain won the battle and we left; my date was evidently displeased. This ended my relationship with the professor's daughter, but not my top grade in geology.

During our free time and before "taps," the soldier-students spent time in the town near the campus. One evening while I was out in town, a middle-aged man (about 40 years of age), introduced himself to me. He gave me his first name, *Michael*, and stated that he was in town to finalize a booking for a classic singer named James Melton. I was familiar with this celebrity; over the past few years I had listened to his impressive baritone voice on Sunday night radio performances, known as, "The Firestone Hour." Michael had convinced me that he was an agent for Mr. Melton. He drove a brand-new convertible; *and* he promised that he would pick me up at my dorm on Sunday to give me a grand tour of the area. He promised to show me the highlights and historical points, going back to the days of George Washington and the Revolutionary War. Believe it or not, he kept his word, and asked me to make an afternoon visit to the home of a Princeton faculty member named, Dr. Alexander.

We went to his lovely home, which was located on a prominent street in town. Michael introduced me as an ASTP student at Princeton. Dr. Alexander was a rather good host and offered us drinks at his expensive bar; although at the time, I was completely unacquainted with alcohol. He apologized for the serious illness of his wife who remained in an upstairs bedroom.

After about 15 minutes of discussion, Michael excused himself to run a quick errand. He stated that he would be back shortly and simply left the home. Dr. Alexander and I continued to chat; he inquired about my college program, and I explained the highlights of the ASTP program. I was convinced that he was probably already aware of the program and its highlights, but throughout the discussion, I decided to go into further detail anyway. At this point in the program we were completing a course in calculus. He asked in-depth questions regarding the course, and I simply responded by stating that the course was at an advanced level and rather complex for him to understand. He humbly accepted my explanation and we proceeded with the discussion about campus history until Michael returned. After a few more minutes we decided to leave; Dr. Alexander shook my hand and wished me good luck during my military career.

Back in the car, Michael was eager to hear my opinion on my visit with Dr. Alexander. I told him that I was rather generic while discussing certain topics; I felt like I could not fully discuss details regarding my calculus program with Dr. Alexander. Michael paused; giving me a strange look. He then informed me that Dr. Alexander was a prominent mathematician and part of Dr. Einstein's mathematical team. At this point, I was completely embarrassed. I felt my height shrinking to about two to three inches high. To this day, I still feel a sense of embarrassment whenever my thoughts turn to Dr. Alexander. *70+ years later*, even as I write this, I feel ashamed and I wish that I could sincerely apologize.

Michael contacted me again about one week later. He invited me to his apartment for an afternoon of coffee and snacks. In addition, he invited me to stay overnight. Since I was a bit skeptical, I asked my dorm roommate, Norm, to join me. The afternoon went well; nothing out of the ordinary, and overall a fun time.

In contrast, the evening arrangement became rather suspicious; especially when Norm and I were told that we would sleep in Michael's bedroom.

Lady Luck intervened when a male friend of his (from New York City) arrived and received priority to sleep with him. This was my first exposure to homosexuality. Next morning, we left his home quickly and quietly, returned to the campus, and never saw Michael again.

Outstanding Education Provided

My engineering program at Princeton continued until January 1944, when the federal government made a final decision to cancel all of the ASTP programs nationwide. Before the closing, my new friend, Norman, and I took advantage of an opportunity to spend some time in New York City. We saw various tourist sites, including evenings at the Stage Door Canteen; where many entertainment celebrities appeared, waited on tables, and performed for the Army, Navy and Marines.

On several Saturday evenings we rode the subway to Coney Island and spent hours testing the rides. On one particular night, after several consecutive rides on the "Cyclone," Norm's stomach became upset, causing him to "upchuck" and spray passengers in the rear seats. A huge apology was given at the end of the ride. I cannot imagine how disgusted they must have felt. It was an unfortunate and repulsive experience.

We stayed at an off-Broadway hotel named, The Palace. It was low-priced and perfectly fit our budget. One night, near the registration desk, I noticed a group of young women waiting and communicating amongst each other in the lobby.

With our room key in hand, we headed for the elevator to reach our 7th floor room. As we passed the ladies, they smiled at us and we returned the compliment with a nod and smile in return. Being young and naive, we were not immediately aware that they were "ladies of the evening" and anxious to earn fees for an "evening's work."

After entering our room, we decided it was time to freshen up before taking the subway back to Coney Island. While I was shaving in the bathroom, Norm answered a knock on the door; when he opened it, one of the "ladies" from the lobby entered and proceeded to lie on the bed. Her first words were, "So, when does the party begin?" After a quick and nervous discussion with Norm, I said, "It is an inconvenient time, as we have an appointment at Coney Island." After a bit of laughter and astonishment, she began to leave but said, "I will be waiting for you in the lobby when you return." With a great feeling of relief, we left within a few minutes and quickly passed through the lobby and headed to the subway.

Outstanding Education Provided

Our evening of entertainment on the amusement park rides went well, and at about 9:00 pm, I suggested that we return to our overnight accommodations. To my surprise, Norm said he was going to make a side trip to the Bronx, to make a brief visit to his relatives living there. He said that he would meet me at our hotel room around midnight. I agreed to this plan and returned to the hotel by myself with a very nervous feeling. The ladies were still waiting for "dates" and I went directly to the elevator without even looking in their direction. Upon entering the room, I immediately locked the door. After a few minutes, I decided to go to bed, but I could not fall asleep right away because I was still nervous and a bit frightened about getting another unexpected knock on the door. What would I do or say if the "lady" returned? About every 15 minutes, I opened the door just a crack to scan up and down the hall. I was awake, completely confused and rather upset at 1:30 in the morning when Norm *finally* returned. The "lady" must have found herself a new customer, because she did not return during the night.

Not long after, mid-morning, we decided to catch the Princeton train for our return. After 19 years of age, I truly began to realize that a whole new world was opening up to me. There were more new experiences to come.

Other weekend passes included sightseeing visits to Washington D.C., where we visited the many memorials; the White House, the U.S. Capital Building, the Washington Monument, the Lincoln Memorial, the Jefferson Memorial, and the Smithsonian Museum.

We even had the opportunity to visit a Russian night club, where we became acquainted with Russian music and culture. The entertainment was delightful and a completely new musical experience for me. I enjoyed the sweet, beautiful sounds of the marvelous Russian instrument called the Balalaika; along with the unforgettable and inspiring music of the Russian classical composer named, Tchaikovsky. From then on, my knowledge of classical musical background has only expanded and improved. Classical music had now definitely become my favorite musical type of expression.

Outstanding Education Provided

After one year, I officially completed my Princeton Engineering Program and received my engineering certification.

The ASTP (Army Specialized Training Program) was discontinued by the United States Department of War; in January, 1944, all G.I. participants were reassigned as PFC's (Private First Class) to active infantry divisions throughout the world, even though the expectation had been that we would graduate as lieutenants.

5. Reassignment to Tennessee

After one full year of army service, believe it or not, I still did not have a single day of basic training. This lack of experience and training came to a crashing conclusion in January, 1944 when I received an army general order. I was assigned to the 78th Infantry Division. I traveled by military train from Princeton, New Jersey, to Camp Butner, North Carolina. Upon arrival there, I reported to division headquarters and was immediately assigned to Co. B, 303rd Medical Battalion. It was earmarked as the medical company serving the medical needs of the 310th Infantry Regiment (one of three regiments in the 78th Division).

I immediately reported to Co. B and I presented my official orders to First Sergeant, Eugene Handsman, in the Company command post. Staff

Staff Sergeant Robert Strusa

29

Reassignment to Tennessee

Sergeant Robert Strusa (a medical technician) was also present, and in the middle of having a casual discussion with him. Sergeant Handsman examined my orders to report to Co. B; while reading my official orders, he noticed that my hometown was Buffalo, New York. When I confirmed this, Sergeant Strusa was curious and started asking me about my Buffalo address. Soon enough, we were both immensely surprised to discover that we were practically neighbors and lived just two blocks apart from each other (in the Riverside area). We were not acquainted with each other back at home simply because of the age gap between us. My current age was 20 and his was 32; thus, we traveled in different social age groups. However, he did know my father, through his barber shop. My father apparently cut his hair regularly. As a result of this "close home" situation, Sergeant Strusa and I became close friends in Co. B.

Since Sergeant Strusa's passing in 1988, I have remained in close contact with his son, Daniel, his daughter, Barbara and his grandson, Joseph (and several other of his family members). Joseph Elliott, Strusa's grandson, a member of U.S. Border Guard, dedicated many hours to researching military records for the military awards, inspired by his grandfather and myself. Due to his diligence we both received a bronze star award for our dedication and bravery in combat while under fire.

As mentioned before, Sergeant Strusa was a medical technician (surgical nurse) in Co. B. I became the company clerk, under Company Commander John Ashby and Sergeant Handsman. I was assigned to a typical army barracks with upper and lower bunks holding 30 Co. B non-commissioned men from the company roster. I was appointed as company clerk because I had completed business school in Buffalo; moreover, I had typing, accounting, and other office experience.

I was only at Camp Butner one week when we were assigned with the entire 78th Division, (along with the 106th Division) to Tennessee, near Murfreesboro, for 6 weeks of army maneuvers. The 106th Division was designated as the *blue army* and the 78th Division was the *red army*. These maneuvers were a simulation of actual battle situations, which could potentially be experienced when we entered the European theater of war, in only months to come.

Upon arrival in the Murfreesboro vicinity, we camped in a heavily wooded area, near the Cumberland River. We were instructed to pitch two-man tents for sleeping. I was stunned – I did not know the first thing about pitching such a tent. I was in the process of making a feeble attempt when Earl Stapp noticed my ineptness. He was about 15 years older than me and had served in the army service in the beginning of the war in 1941. He was transferred to Co. B, my medical unit, in 1943, and lost his sergeant stripes prior to his transfer. I never questioned the reason behind that, because he was an immensely considerate soldier, and left a good impression by immediately assisting me when I needed help.

With his assistance and a miniscule amount of help from me, the tent was completed. He shared the tent with me and we shared our blankets inside the tent. He pointed out that the trick to successfully pitching a tent was digging a small trench around the perimeter of the tent. Due to immaturity and lack of basic training, I did not even think to consider that the trench would come in handy, during rainfall. The trench would serve to divert rainwater and spare soldiers from sleeping on cold and wet blankets.

The two of us shared a tent throughout our entire Tennessee maneuver and we continued to have a father-son relationship until the conclusion of the war. He was 34 years of age and I was 21. We remained very friendly after the Tennessee experience and throughout the forthcoming war battles in Germany. He was home-raised in Arkansas. I was very impressed with his personality, maturity, military experiences, and most of all his southern accent.

While on maneuvers, our food supply consisted of K-rations (3 daily). Since maneuvers took a period of about one month, the meals became extremely boring and monotonous. One day, Stapp asked me if I wanted a full southern corn fried chicken dinner. I was immensely excited about this, thinking "finally, something different to eat," although I must say I was slightly puzzled as to where he was going to obtain these dinners.

Reassignment to Tennessee

He asked me to take a walk with him; we went down a dirt road in a wooded area, and came to a farmhouse, with a full front porch outside of the door. Sitting on rockers on the porch were a hillbilly, his wife and son. The scenario reminded me of a scene in the movie *Deliverance*, when several hunters came across a house of a similar mood.

Sergeant Stapp, being from the South and all, immediately greeted the residents with a cheerful "Howdy," and started a conversation. After a few words, he very diplomatically mentioned that we were hungry and were longing for a southern corn fried chicken dinner. The hint was promptly accepted by the family, and I could not believe that with such ease, we actually were invited to stay for a full-course chicken dinner. The dinner was *delicious*, absolutely delicious. We were encouraged to take the leftovers back to our camp area. There was no need to ask us twice.

Our maneuvers with the 106th Infantry Division went well, with the help of officers and judges making productive decisions regarding the specific tactics of the red and blue armies and simulated casualties. Honestly, the maneuvers went as well as could be expected, the only downside was that the snow rates were above average that February. I cannot be too bitter about that, simply because this type of weather prepared us for similar weather that we would encounter in Germany from December, 1944 to March, 1945.

6.   Camp Pickett—Combat Training

When Tennessee maneuvers concluded in March, 1944, the 78th Division left for a new home in Camp Pickett, Virginia. There we were billeted in the usual Army barracks – 30 enlisted men; and the first sergeant (Sergeant Handsman) who had his own small, private room in the front of the building.

While at Camp Pickett, we would regularly do ten and twenty-mile hikes to build up our endurance and strength. The hikes were beyond tiring, but I surprisingly made it through them, and became a much stronger and better soldier as a result.

There were other duties that had to be assigned such as kitchen police (KP), guard duty (2-hour shifts), vehicle cleaning, barracks housekeeping, and so forth. Since I was appointed as company clerk, I was given the uncomfortable task of assigning

The Author at Camp Pickett

company privates and privates first class to do these tasks. I used an official duty roster to ensure fairness and equal work loads to all. I was a private first class up until this point, but then I was promoted to corporal, which gave me the authority to make these assignments. There were no complaints, so I assumed that I was making fair and equal assignments to all.

Co. B was similar to all the other infantry companies regarding religious diversity. With a chapel on the grounds, all religions were recognized at different times during the weekends. However, there were always a few religious G.I.'s that directed teasing remarks toward Southern Baptists and other minority religions, sometimes insensitively called "Holy Rollers."

One such incident occurred at Camp Pickett; when a few members of Co. B decided to paint the shower wall (7x9) with a full colored mural of a naked mermaid. The intended member of Co. B (victim in my opinion) went to take a shower, and when he disrobed and entered the shower, a loud scream was heard. He furiously ran out of the shower, and then out of the building, in the nude. He could not be found anywhere in the area or anywhere on the camp, *and* he left his clothes behind.

After several hours of searching, the company commander of Co. B called the Military Police and declared him "absent without leave" (AWOL). He never returned to Co. B and was never heard from again.

The mural painters were identified and sentenced to two weeks of KP and guard duty, followed by 100 laps around the camp grounds. I just could not believe that human beings could be so cruel and insensitive to their fellow man.

The 78th Division remained at Camp Pickett through the summer months of 1944. It was a very hot and humid summer for those of us in Southern Virginia. In late July, General Parker, the commanding officer of the entire division, ordered a mandatory division inspection of *all* the division units. It was to take place on a wide-open area, referred to as the parade grounds.

All units of the 78th Division were assembled on the grounds in full uniform dress; wearing field packs, helmets, boots, and other *heavy* woolen clothing. All soldiers were assembled in full military order, in extensive long lines. Not only did the full uniform feel like it was weighing me down, but it was just so unbelievably hot outside too. The heat reached an immensely oppressive 105 degrees.

The general asked to have his favorite waltz played by the division band during his inspection of the troops. All were standing at attention and remained at attention during the entire troop review, while the popular waltz of the time "Alice Blue Gown" was played over and over again.

I began to feel very uncomfortable and faint from the heat and prayed that I wouldn't collapse in a heap in front of the commanding general. I was not alone in the suffering and approaching collapse. As I took a quick glance down the lines of troops, I noticed some bodies that had fallen to the ground; mostly infantry regiment members, due to the extra equipment that they were wearing. I felt that "Alice Blue Gown" would never end. It was simply excruciating that in addition, it was played as an *encore* over and over and over again.

When the review of the troops was concluded, the collapsed G.I.'s were doused with water as their heavy equipment was removed. It was such a relieving moment. All of the men were safely revived; but the remainder of our stay at Camp Pickett was remembered as the "Alice Blue Gown Army Training Center."

The remaining summer days were spent in preparation and training for dangerous problems that could potentially be encountered on our anticipated transportation to the European Theater of War. My military experience began in January 1943, and *at last* in July 1944, I was to receive military basic training, which was essential before confronting the German enemy on the European continent. I was still totally untrained about how to conduct and protect myself in combat conditions.

One early morning in July 1944, my entire company and I were taken to a very well-designed basic training area at Camp Pickett; it included walls to climb, ropes to swing on over land and water obstacles, barbed wire to crawl under, and live gunfire to avoid.

With typical beginner problems, I did manage to handle these challenges with a fair degree of success and confidence. During the first test of courage and wit, we were asked to crawl under about fifty yards of low-hanging barbed wire with *live* machine gun fire taking place. The shots were first being aimed across the course about one foot above our prone bodies struggling forward on the rough ground as we tried to avoid being entangled in the barbed wire.

I proceeded across the course and under the wire, and to my surprise, I somehow progressed on my stomach under this barbed wire course without panic and nervousness. The adrenaline kept me moving. My primary thought was to keep my head, legs and butt very close to the Earth to avoid being struck by the live ammunition flying by (closely) overhead.

When I reached the middle of the course, I encountered another G.I. trainee who was laying motionless and in tears. As he nervously wept, he told me that he could not proceed any further, although the officers in charge of the live bullets whizzing over his head refused to stop the firing. I asked his name and his unit and explained to him that I was also afraid, *terrified* if anything, but at the same time I knew that I *had to* successfully complete the dangerous task.

I poked him in the arm with my feet and asked him to proceed with me along my side. After a few encouraging words from me, we both began our forward movement once again. His courage and stamina seemed to return when he observed my progress.

Upon completion of the course, he thanked me for my support and then was confronted by the officers in charge who gave him a stern lecture regarding his conduct. I was not approached by the officers and my friend suddenly disappeared without an opportunity for me to get his name.

Upon return to my army unit, I expressed my appreciation to my commanding officer for being subjected to this dangerous combat obstacle course, which greatly increased my courage and ability to handle similar combat conditions in the future. Similar combat situations were going to develop in the very near future during the Battle of the Bulge.

This obstacle course incident, where I was able to positively influence another frightened G.I., was an immensely strong psychological and emotional occurrence in my military career. My naivety was disappearing, while my maturity in the military and in life was becoming much more developed. I realized that God was watching out for me and my future. My combat experiences to occur in the very near future were to be carried out without fear of danger or death.

On a lighter note; while at Camp Pickett, I was given weekend passes to Washington, D.C. and Fredericksburg, Virginia. My weekend tours to these cities are exceptionally memorable to me. I visited all of the beautiful memorials, the Capital, and the White House. In Fredericksburg, I had the wonderful opportunity to visit the U.S.O. and to be entertained by the attractive young ladies who had volunteered to make me and hundreds of other soldiers feel at home. This included attending theater presentations, dancing, and enjoying dinners with fine companionship.

7.　　Life on the Atlantic

Unfortunately, basic training came to an end too soon when the 78th Division received military orders to move to Fort Dix, New Jersey to prepare for embarkation overseas.

We received medical examinations, syringe injections (to avoid prevalent diseases), and new clothing, including helmets, field packs, and first aid supplies. We received a full introduction regarding what dangers to expect in combat areas and proper actions to take to ensure and maintain our safety in the face of Nazi military action.

A few days before boarding our ship, the *John Erickson*, which was built a few years earlier in Sweden; I developed a neck infection, which became a very large boil (medically called a carbuncle). It was excruciatingly painful, especially when training or moving my neck in any direction.

On October 14, 1944, we left Fort Dix for the boarding pier in New York City. We were to be departing for England. The army field pack was strapped across my shoulders and its weight had a very painful effect on the carbuncle area. I cannot even describe how uncomfortable it was. We arrived at the pier in the evening and were greeted by a cheery Army marching band. I recall the band playing patriotic music, including the inspiring march "Over There" composed by George M. Cohan. It was an impressive way to wish us "Bon Voyage" and a safe return home after the conclusion of the war.

Life on the Atlantic

As we passed by the band and began to climb up the gangplank my pain became worse and I almost slipped as I was boarding. In my painful condition, I remember muttering, "Stop the damn music!"

Of course, it continued, as I made my way up to the main deck of the ship, alongside my fellow medics. Once we were upon the ship, we were guided to our "staterooms," which we discovered were on the eighth and *lowest* deck on the ship. We were shocked to see that our beds were hammocks, 6 tiers high; the clearance between the tiers (when occupied) was roughly less than three inches. Our entire battalion (four companies consisting of over 250 individuals) were the occupants of this lowest level of the ship.

Several of us commented that this level was overly crowded and that the temperature was way too warm. We also realized that if a German U-Boat (enemy submarine) torpedoed us in the Atlantic Ocean, the torpedoes would hit directly over our level and the entire battalion would be destroyed at sea. Fortunately, we were accompanied by eight navy destroyers and this discouraged action by the submarines.

Once I maneuvered myself into my tight hammock, I realized that my neck pain and the high temperatures were impossible for me to bear through this long ocean trip. My company commander was informed about my medical condition and ordered that I be moved to the sick bay on the top side of the ship for medical attention and minor surgery (to lance the carbuncle).

Sick bay was air-conditioned and filled with daylight. I was given a single bed with fresh, clean sheets and a private bathroom equipped with a fresh water (no salt) shower.

Through the portholes, the Statue of Liberty was clearly seen as the ship left the New York harbor. This was the first time in my life that I had actually seen the statue and it was a very inspiring sight for me as an untrained rookie going into battle against the well-trained Nazi divisions.

I laid in my sick bay recovery bed and wondered what my future held in store for me. I simply could not imagine the death and destruction that was waiting for me within the next few months. However, the view of the Statue of Liberty greatly aroused my sense of patriotism and made me recall the remarkable history of the United States and the great nation that it became.

I recalled the attack on Pearl Harbor, the D-Day invasion of the European continent and all the members of the military that had sacrificed their lives for their country. At this point, I was not sure what was awaiting me, but I felt confident that I could make a notable contribution to help my country succeed.

With all these special and unexpected events occurring as we sailed away from the New York harbor, across the Atlantic Ocean toward an unknown fate, I felt strong and unafraid because I knew that God was watching over me. I prayed that he would minimize the dire worry and concern that my parents were enduring.

For the first few days the ocean voyage was very calm and without incident. I felt a strong sense of guilt while I was resting in sick-bay, while my comrades in Co. B were on the lowest deck in the heat and compact hammocks. This feeling of guilt resulted in my request to the sick bay doctor to let me return to the rest of my medical battalion.

After about a day of trying to convince him that my neck condition had greatly improved, he stated that he would give me permission to return but emphasized that I could stay in sick-bay until we completed our ocean voyage to England. I immediately elected to return to my company.

The next morning, I was escorted to my hammock on the bottom deck. Here, every person complained about the excruciating heat, crowded conditions, and the very realistic fear of being torpedoed. I immediately picked up their concerns and wondered why I was so anxious to return to this situation.

The next day I was asked to see the company commander, Captain John Ashby, in his room. He congratulated me for the wise decision that I had made by returning to my comrades. He had been informed by the master sergeant that all the men in Co. B had developed a high degree of respect for me when I made the decision to return and suffer uncomfortably with them down below.

After another day, the master sergeant told me that I was assigned the duty of removing the garbage from the lowest deck and climbing up a long flight of stairs to the main deck, to toss the garbage over the railing and into the ocean.

I had developed a severe case of seasickness down in the lower deck and only felt well in a prone position on my hammock. The garbage had to be carried to the top deck, but my condition was getting worse and I felt that I could not climb all the steps needed to reach the top deck. The nausea was truly overwhelming.

I needed to give it a try, so I picked up the garbage bags and made a strong attempt to complete my mission.

Seasickness in today's modern technological world is not as big of a hassle for sea voyagers, but in 1944, ships were not nearly as sturdy or smooth-sailing among the ocean waves.

Before I reached the top of the steps, I felt sick to my stomach. I attempted to suppress it with every ounce of power in me. As soon as I opened the top-deck, I made a very quick sprint for the railing, and without any hesitation, I threw the bag out to the sea with all my strength. To my surprise, it did not fall into the sea, but was held in the air by the wind and very slowly began floating toward the bow of the ship. As I observed its forward movement, I noticed that there were three top army officers standing at the rail, downwind from my position. Due to my seasickness, I was not able to remain in my position for more than a few seconds, just long enough to see that the bags full of garbage were caught by the wind and headed directly toward them! With my last glance before heading down into the hold, I saw the officers completely covered with this waste. I left them with looks of pure confusion and outrage on their faces.

Fortunately, they did not recognize the source of this contamination and I successfully made it down to the lowest deck; however, I was left worrying about the incident for the entire remaining voyage across the Atlantic Ocean.

As we approached the English Channel, the great concern about being torpedoed by Nazi U-Boats became an even more serious concern and we were ordered to wear life jackets for the remainder of the ocean trip.

8.   Arrival in England

On October 26, 1944, with our destroyer escort we made it safely and without incident to Southampton on the southern English coast, where we disembarked the next morning. We were delighted to finally leave our "comfortable" hammocks and the heat and stuffiness of the lower deck. We were ordered to dress in full military and combat uniforms to make a good impression on the English population living in the nearby area.

Upon debarkation we immediately were transported by train to other nearby communities for an unspecified time. Our destination was a quaint English town named Christchurch, where we were billeted in the Mudeford area.

As we approached the town, I noticed that the nearby coastal beaches were covered with barbed wire and a great variety of explosives. This had all been in place since the beginning of the war and a result of the heavy air bombing of the English cities and towns, particularly London. The possibility of a Nazi channel invasion was a great concern and all precautions were taken.

I learned that just a few miles outside of Christchurch was a military airfield with many camouflaged bomber war planes. The planes made daily bombing missions over Germany to destroy munitions factories.

Arrival in England

During the few weeks that we remained in Christchurch, I heard the loud sounds of the aircraft with their courageous flight crews, taking off for their German bombing targets. Although the German population was a part of our enemy, I found myself greatly concerned about their safety and the dangerous lives they had to endure. I felt especially compassionate for the children who were innocent and not even a part of this total devastating war. I wished there was some way to guarantee the safety of all the innocent, but life is not always so ideal.

As we approached the area where Co. B would set up to provide medical services to the 310th Infantry Regiment, our conversations with the local English citizens made me aware of some of the distinct language differences. For instance, a truck is known as a *lorry*, a bar is a *pub*, hood of car/truck is a *bonnet*, the trunk is the *boot*, gas is *petrol*, and sneakers are known as *plimsoll*.

The homes in Christchurch were quite modern and updated in comparison to the homes in Buffalo. Although after the war ended and I returned home, I did notice that home builders were catching up to the English builders.

When we entered the home that we would remain in for the next few weeks, I was slow in finding a sleeping area for myself. The bedrooms were taken, the sofas were full and I had to find a leftover. The only place left turned out to be the island work counter in the kitchen. I unrolled my bedroll on it and that was officially my permanent bed. It was unusual, but comfortable.

While we were in the Christchurch area, we received new clothing and equipment to help us survive when we crossed the English Channel. We went on daily hikes and runs to keep in good physical condition. During one of our hikes, we noticed a pub located at the water's edge and we were invited by the local residents to visit there in the evening.

I, with my naivety still apparent, thought I was going to a public building to learn about social life and entertainment in southern England. Much to my surprise, I discovered local citizens and American military at a long bar drinking the English beer called

Arrival in England

Guinness. At the piano was an older woman in a black witch costume, entertaining the room.

It was late October and it turns out the piano entertainer's outfit was actually the bad witch costume from the movie *The Wizard of Oz.* At first sight, I had assumed that this was her everyday dress, but I had forgotten that Halloween was a few days away.

Here, the popular form of entertainment was not cards or dice games, but rather the game of Darts. After observing the game for some time, I decided to challenge the current champion. I found the game very interesting and much to my surprise, I was a worthy opponent and challenger.

During the course of the evening, the "piano witch" continued to sing and play excellent WWII tunes. Some of these tunes were "Bluebirds Over the White Cliffs of Dover," "When the Lights Go On Again All Over the World," and "Lili Marlene" (a German song).

The pianist also played an off-color tune called "Roll Me Over and Do It Again." This naive 20-year-old veteran was somewhat shocked and embarrassed, but I realized that it was an everyday, popular tune that helped relieve the tension and anxiety of the English people and English soldiers.

My short military experience in Christchurch, England was a very memorable and educational one, although there was an unusual atmosphere due to the war and invasion fears and concerns. There was a very nearby military airfield just outside of the town and takeoff and landing sounds could be heard at anytime, day or night. Bombing flights into Germany were being made on a very regular schedule.

The one environmental difference to me was the beautiful beach area on the southern English Channel coast. This beach and coastal area, which was always enjoyed by the local residents, was no longer available for swimming, sunning and beach sports, because it had been totally covered with many miles of barbed wire and land mines. All of this was to prevent and deter a German invasion across the English Channel. This defensive and protective situation had been in place since 1939 and removed upon German surrender in May, 1945.

Arrival in England

The local citizens were very cooperative and friendly to the American military force. The residents and families, local businessmen and government officials were respectful and understanding as they knew the American presence was only temporary. The task ahead, for us and many others, was the invasion of Germany.

9. Crossing the English Channel

In my short stay there, I grew to know the life and culture of the British citizenry. Our short encampment on the southern British coast came to an end in the middle of November 1944. We were moved by military trucks to an embarkation point at Portland, England, a few miles from Christchurch. There we boarded landing craft vessels (LST), the same that were used in the D-Day invasion at Omaha Beach on June 6, 1944. These vessels were of an absolute no-frill nature. There was no place to sit except on the deck floor while wearing full battle gear, which included field packs, life preservers, helmets and combat boots.

The voyage across the English Channel took about four hours and was extremely uncomfortable, with very tight quarters holding as many GI's as possible. The Channel crossing was also rough due to the inclement weather conditions in November. This resulted in an additional unexpected and unpleasant disadvantage—seasickness with the usual side effect.

After these totally uncomfortable hours, we finally crossed to Le Havre, a French seaport on the Seine River. Then on November 23, 1944, we continued down the Seine to the city of Rouen.

At this point we disembarked and walked as a group about one mile to the local railroad yard, where a train with a large number of boxcars was waiting for us. The boarding process was well-organized, and we were assigned to particular boxcars as a unit. These boxcars were called "40 or 8's" which meant that each car held either 40 military persons or eight horses (which were used and needed at the German front lines).

Through the open boxcar door, I could see that the floor was totally covered with straw. When I inquired about the reason, I was told that it had just previously transported eight horses and the straw (which was obviously important for the horses) had not been removed. We had to sleep on the straw and make the best out of it, even though no one had any knowledge of what the horses had left under the straw. After some moments of repulsion, I accepted the situation, since I truly had no choice. I unrolled my sleeping bag in a corner of the car, gritted my teeth and learned to accept the odors.

Before the train left for Germany, trucks came along the rail platform and tossed (onto the freight car) enough cases of K-Rations to provide us with food and drinks until our journey was complete. The K-Rations should have consisted of individual cases of breakfast, lunch and dinner. Breakfast included cans of packaged eggs, muffins, and juice. Lunch included American cheese slabs, bread, and fruit juice. Dinner included a can of beef, pork, or chicken, with juice and cookies.

This would have been satisfactory and tolerable for the three-day journey across France, Belgium and into Germany, except for a bad mistake made by the delivery military men. Instead of including breakfast, lunch and dinner cases, they accidentally supplied only lunch cases of cheese for all three daily meals. By the time of our arrival in Germany, I could not stomach and eat cheese anymore. As a result, I found all cheese particularly distasteful and could not eat or smell cheese for decades after the war ended.

After three days, we arrived near Yvetot, France, where we left the train and bivouacked from November 23 to November 27, 1944. An extraordinarily delicious Thanksgiving dinner was served on November 24. This was an immensely memorable feast and quite the morale boost.

10. German Combat Begins

On November 29th we boarded military trucks to our next destination, Tongres, Belgium, near Aachen, Germany, a city near the Belgian border that had been totally demolished by American and British air raids.

Here we were supplied with cans of food, called spam, that were well-known but not relished by G.I.'s. This, I believe is still available in grocery stores at the present time, but never purchased by military personnel who had to consume it during the war. Thankfully, this was a temporary inconvenience until we were transported to Roetgen, Germany on December 7.

On December 13th, the 310th Regiment began its first attack at the front line, along with the total 78th Infantry Division near the Ruhr River in western Germany. Co. B of the 303rd Medical Battalion was stationed in the German town of Lammersdorf. We occupied a very small hotel, which had been badly damaged by air strikes and artillery shelling. This was established as our first medical and surgical station on the front battle line.

Co. B was attached to the 310th Infantry Regiment; one of three regiments included in the 78th Division. Co. B ambulances were strategically placed behind the medical station and were used constantly to transport the injured infantrymen from the nearby front line to our medical station. Here, they received limited medical and surgical aid before being transported by ambulance to a field hospital

German Combat Begins

(about ten miles behind the front lines), like the field hospital seen in the TV program of many years called "MASH."

In Lammersdorf, Germany, our company kitchens and cooks provided all company personnel with good and healthy meals, three times each day. Thankfully, K-rations and Spam were no longer our food source.

One room in the Lammersdorf building was sealed off and used as a combat surgical and medical area by our company commander, Captain Andrew Heath (a surgical doctor), and the four surgical technicians assisting him. Captain Heath was a replacement for Captain John Ashby who was transferred to the 303rd Battalion Headquarters Company. These four members of Co. B were staff sergeants and were indispensable in assisting Captain Heath. Our surgical unit not only assisted in giving surgical and medical aid to infantrymen, but also assisted those with mental and psychological problems (because of heavy German shelling and tank attacks during the Battle of the Bulge). Occasionally, a few injured German soldiers who were recently wounded and captured within our general battle area were also administered to, although they were prisoners of war. Many expressed their gratitude for medical care that they assumed that they were not entitled to as enemy soldiers.

I was not part of the surgical and medical team, but instead continued as company clerk, responsible to the company first sergeant and the company commander. Communication between infantry divisions, regiments and battalions was an absolute necessity in order to provide smooth, accurate and successful movements.

We were now a major unit in the Battle of the Bulge. The Nazi troops had penetrated into Belgium and made a final and major attempt to make the Allied forces retreat, hopefully, all the way back to the English Channel and the Atlantic Ocean. This was the last offensive drive of the German Army before complete surrender. Therefore, in addition to my duties as company clerk, I received the additional duty as courier between the Co. B Medical Unit and the 310th Regimental Battalion Headquarters, located just about two miles down the road near a German town named Schmitt.

German Combat Begins

This required a daily morning ride with the Jeep driver, to deliver daily accurate reports regarding Co. B medical services, and a return trip with a large sealed envelope containing vital information about troop movements of the 78th Division and other divisions in the area. These daily trips to update our company commander were essential to make the German Bulge retreat a positive and continuing one.

During our Tennessee maneuvers a few months earlier, our make-believe enemy was the 106th Division. The 106th Division arrived in the same general area in Germany as the 78th Division, just a few miles southwest of our division.

As fate would have it, the Germans made their major forward Bulge push with many tanks, strong artillery, and many foot soldiers through the area being maintained by the 106th Division, and annihilated two of the three regiments that were in the path of the German juggernaut. Thousands of infantrymen died or were severely wounded by this German surprise attack.

The 78th Division was not in the direct path of the German offensive drive and held their ground with significantly fewer casualties. It was immensely difficult for me and the other 78th Division members to accept and realize the terrible fate that befell the 106th Division whom we maneuvered against in Tennessee. To this day, it is still a terribly upsetting memory.

My daily regimental correspondence trips with my Jeep driver continued without incident throughout the month of December, 1944, until December 21st, when fate and luck entered the outcome of the daily trip to the regimental headquarters.

The German army was now being pushed back; the German tanks were running out of gasoline, and the cold winter weather and snow had a very discouraging effect on German manpower and military equipment. As a result, my daily courier duty became vital as our offensive military movements were making more progress. It was essential that all regimental units were unified and acting in accordance with one another, as well as with other Army divisions in the Bulge area.

On the morning of December 21st, I was seated in the Jeep along with the driver to make, what I assumed, would be my daily routine round trip. At that exact moment of departure, the Co. B company commander, Captain Andrew Heath, rushed out of the building and asked very seriously and with authority for me to get out of the Jeep.

He stated that he was making the short trip there personally because there was a very reliable rumor that there was a major movement planned for this day that would involve all the Army divisions in the vicinity and that this would crush and eliminate the German Bulge finally and permanently.

Without hesitation, he ordered the driver to proceed immediately with him in command. As they departed I was left standing by our surgical base wondering what this was all about.

I reentered the building and returned to

Captain Andrew Heath

my post in the command headquarters. After only a few moments, I heard noise and shouts outside where I had seen the company commander leave. Upon inquiry, I was told that a German 88 shell had made a direct hit on the Jeep. The bodies of Captain Heath and the driver were being brought back. Upon return, there was no question that they were both killed *instantly*.

At that moment, and on many, many occasions long after WWII ended, I have reflected on this day and questioned why I was spared. Even now, eight decades after the conclusion of the war, in my retirement years, I wonder why this tragic event took place, especially after learning that the rumor that precipitated this tragic event was *absolutely false*. My mind could not accept the tragedy that, in my opinion, was meant for me. I cried without shame when the bodies arrived. I rushed into our building, went to a rear unoccupied room, found a corner, slid down the corner wall with my head between my knees and cried out loud, just like a small child.

I was asking God and myself for an answer for the unforgettable event that had just occurred. To this date, the only explanation that I could accept was that God had other plans for me in my later and adult years. I have relived this terrible tragedy over and over during the ensuing 72 plus years, since I continue to communicate with Captain Heath's daughter, Margaret, on a regular basis. She was only two years old at the time of his death. I have received several military photos of Captain Heath, which I have displayed in my home office.

This incident gave me a sense of confidence, security and maturity that helped me find balance within my military career. My naive attitudes that were part of me when I was inducted were gone because of this experience; but I knew that in the future God was at my back and watching over me. This became very apparent during my future combat missions in Germany.

With Christmas 1944 just days away, war efforts became quiet and we were all anticipating a wonderful Christmas dinner. This anticipation turned into a beautiful reality. On Christmas Eve, we were treated to a very special event. As a surprise the Medical Battalion had received a special movie film from the 78th Division headquarters. The members of the 303rd Medical Battalion were invited to the command post of our medical headquarters company to see and enjoy the movie in the uppermost, unoccupied level of their building. Although I am not certain, it appeared to be an attic used for storage purposes. The space was limited; therefore, the film could only be shown to the personnel of one company at a time. Co. B was fortunate to see it on Christmas Eve, 1944.

There was not very comfortable seating, but it was still an incredibly pleasant experience. The film was quite fit for the Christmas season. It was a newly produced film entitled "The Song of Bernadette," starring Jennifer Jones as a religious French girl in the

1800's who had a vision of the Virgin Mary. This became an Oscar-winning film and it made a profound effect on all who were viewing it.

While the movie was being shown, the roar of German V-1 rockets could be heard flying overhead. We were informed that as long as the roar continued, the rocket would not explode nearby. The ultimate destination of these rockets was London, England. The German war machine was also perfecting a more sophisticated and dangerous rocket called the V-2; but these were not fully operational at this time. The roar of the V-1 rockets became more and more noticeable as the film was being shown on the screen; the members of Co. B became tense and nervous. The roars were taunting and provoked paranoia, leading the men to constantly wonder whether these roars would cease and if a rocket would suddenly explode nearby.

Fortunately, the rockets continuously flew beyond our area and exploded in distant places, perhaps Brussels or London. The beautiful film was an unforgettable Christmas Eve experience, only marred by the frightening thought of the building being destroyed and Army personnel being injured or killed. To this day, I view this film without fail whenever it becomes available.

Christmas Day was quiet and peaceful because both the Americans and Germans totally respected the holiness of the day. The kitchen personnel in some lucky way received all the delicious components necessary to comprise a complete Christmas dinner. The entire group of Co. B personnel thoroughly enjoyed the blessed Christmas Day in 1944.

As New Year's Eve approached, the surgical technicians who assisted the new, temporary company commander, John Ashby, decided to make it an appropriate New Year's Eve function. Since there was no alcohol of any kind available for New Year toasts, the surgical technicians decided to *improvise* by using surgical alcohol and mixing it with fresh fallen snow to craft drinkable, alcoholic toasts for 1945. As I tell this 1945 New Year's Eve incident to my present-day friends, most find it very difficult to believe.

I cannot comment on the quality of these cocktails because I did not imbibe at this point in my life. Alcohol had never touched my lips at age 21. The other Co. B, noncommissioned, enlisted men, apparently were not as innocent and naive as myself. The drinks were distributed, and noise and gaiety began.

After about one hour, I heard sobbing in one of the other rooms. When I went to investigate, I discovered that it came from the Co. B drill sergeant, who was known for his aggressiveness towards privates and privates first class. In training they *all* cowered before him in fear when he gave orders and commands. I remember his name but I will not reveal it at this time for his sake. The sergeant was slouched down in a corner of the room with a surgical alcohol cocktail in his hand, and he was muttering out loud, "I want my mommy!" There is no need to say that all of those that heard this, no longer respected him as a Co. B leader. However, I now recognized him as a genuine human being and not as a belligerent bully.

He remembered upon sobering up the next morning that I had seen and heard him in this embarrassing situation. His treatment of me was respectful and friendly from that day until the end of the war. This was an unforgettable New Year's Eve and it remains an immensely vivid memory in my mind to this day, seven decades later.

Co. B.'s medical assistance continued in Lammersdorf until January 10, 1945; during this time, medical personnel were busy with many medical and surgical procedures.

In addition, the cold winter storms and blizzards did not abate. During this period, we were visited by several members of the military police who had an AWOL (absent without leave) private in their custody and were ordered to bring him to our company for reassignment.

We learned that he had gone AWOL several times before and that he had spent several months in an Army stockade (military prison) prior to his arrival here. After an indoctrination with the company commander and the first sergeant, he was given a place to stay and carry out his army duties with Co. B. His first name was Leo. He was belligerent and resentful; but decided to befriend me and ignore the rest of the company.

German Combat Begins

When entering the command post, he did not approach the first sergeant, but always came to get his orders from me. I felt very odd about this and discussed the problem with the first sergeant. He ultimately accepted the situation, as long as Leo was doing his work and not creating a problem.

A day or two went by and the sun came out with a bit of warmer weather, so many G.I.'s decided to absorb some of the nice weather in the fields next to the building where our medical unit was established. While absorbing the sunshine, we suddenly realized that there were several German planes overhead, which began strafing the entire area with their machine guns.

There was a rather deep four-foot drainage ditch along the road in front of the building, and at this point, Leo grabbed me and tossed me into this ditch to avoid the spraying bullets. He also jumped in and partially protected me with his body. It was the logical thing to do and although I was soaked with cold water and melting ice, I thanked Leo and expressed my gratitude for his quick thinking.

Leo's quick thinking saved my life. Once again and for the second time, God smiled upon me. This made me wonder even more about what my future life would hold for me. This episode gave me a better and kinder feeling for Leo and the personal problems that he had and kept locked up inside his mind. Leo had psychological problems probably from childhood to the present time and they were more powerful than he could handle in this combat Army situation. Two days later, he went AWOL again and left no indication of where he was going.

We learned a few days later that he had pilfered a Captain's uniform and had gone by himself into a small German village and visited a German home occupied by a family consisting of a father, mother and two grown daughters. He identified himself as the doctor and company commander and explained that his role there was to inspect for venereal disease. He asked them to take off all their clothes, to completely strip; they complied, with fear of what noncompliance might cost in terms of punishment (from the US Army). After enjoying the sight of four nude, embarrassed and uncomfortable German citizens, he left their residence.

German Combat Begins

The next day, the German father walked to battalion headquarters to discuss the weird event. Immediately upon hearing the story, the battalion commander issued an order for Leo's arrest. This was the reason why Leo went AWOL again and I never saw or heard from him ever again; but I will always remember him for helping spare my life for the second time at Lammersdorf.

About two or three days later, we heard that the military police had once again captured him. When his criminal case was presented to the Army court, he was sentenced to an undetermined sentence at Sing Sing Prison in New York State.

I do not know how many years he had spent in prison, but I did learn (from military records) that he passed away in the 70's, long after the war ended. Prison and war were not the last of his memories. That comforts me, as I recall that I seemed to be his only friend.

11. Army Movement to the Rhine River

Upon return to the command post, I learned that the 78th Division was moving from the Lammersdorf vicinity and driving toward the Rhine river. The Battle of the Bulge was successfully won and the battle for the Rhineland was to begin.

After leaving the Lammersdorf area of Germany and the tragic events there, including the death of our company commander Captain Andrew Heath, we proceeded with the 78th infantry regiments and the engineering battalion, slowly toward the heart of Germany: breaching the last of the Siegfried Line defenses, capturing the West bank of the Ruer River, the military center at Schmitt and gaining control of the Schwammenauel Dam.

The 303rd Medical Battalion was fully prepared to give equal medical attention to the entire 78th Infantry Division, as it did during those cold, harsh and dangerous weeks during the Battle of the Bulge. As our medical vehicles moved slowly and carefully along main roads leading to the City of Bonn and the Ludendorff Bridge at Remagen, we passed through many small German towns and dorfs (villages), that at first glance, seemed to have been spared from major destruction.

We traveled uninterrupted though these German dorfs, until we reached a larger one with somewhat more industry and population than the others that we previously traveled through. Euskirchen was on the main route to Bonn. As our vehicles entered Euskirchen, I noticed that the breadth of war destruction in our assigned area was significantly less in comparison to the other areas that I had previously seen in Euskirchen. Company B was to spend the night here and our newly appointed company commander, Captain Randolph Linhart, arranged for all if us to stay at a park facility noted for its beautiful landscaping.

As we walked down a well-gardened path to our facility, we passed several stone-covered, private picnic areas. To see inside each dark, cave-like area required keen eyesight. While passing these, I heard a quiet moaning from one and without observing caution, I entered it to find the cause.

Sitting on a rear, darkened bench, I noticed an older, white-bearded man in torn, unclean clothes and jacket. I spoke to him in English and he quietly mumbled some words to me in German that I could not understand. I began to leave, and he grasped my arm and began to cry. I realized that he was hungry, cold, and all alone without any help.

I helped him up and walked him out from the closed area into the daylight. The sudden light temporarily bothered his eyes, making him rush back toward the darkness. I called to the first sergeant who was nearby and we supported this man to a medical litter (stretcher) and took him to the building where our surgical and medical technicians were setting up. There, he received food, water and a good body cleaning.

This man was immensely grateful and came directly to me to give his goodbye, *auf wiedersehen*, and thank you before his release to our intelligence unit. The discovery of this poor, cold, delirious soul huddled in this dark, unheated space made me wonder and reflect upon why mankind enters wars that ultimately degrade, humiliate and kill innocent human beings. It's terrible to think about areas of civilization being destroyed by bombs, artillery, tanks, automatic rifles and guns. These victims of war and devastated areas are sympathized with for a few years and then repressed in our memories; and then, humanity is once again ready for the next war, which will have progressively more sophisticated weapons to further humiliate mankind, destroy and perhaps end the world. The poor, frightened and humiliated man that meekly cried out to me for help is only one example of man's inhumanity to man, and I will always carry his image with me until my death.

The next morning our medical unit continued our advance eastward toward the city of Bonn, on the Rhine River. Just before entering Bonn, the entire 78th Division moved southward along Route 9, leading to Remagen, Germany.

The German army was fully aware that the Rhine River was the final natural barrier to prevent the U.S. and English armies from reaching Berlin. The allied armies were invading Germany from the west, while the Russian army was invading from the east. The German troops and Luftwaffe were determined to keep the U.S. troops from crossing the Rhine River. The Germans destroyed all but one of the Rhine River bridges. They did this by attaching explosives to the bridges and bombing by the Luftwaffe.

The Ludendorff Railroad Bridge, also

Ludendorff Bridge at Remagen

known as the Remagen Bridge, was the only one remaining on the entire river. For some unknown reason, the explosives attached to the bridge did not cause the bridge to collapse; although they did greatly weaken the bridge so that it swayed and trembled intensely as the Allied Forces slowly approached.

The 78th Infantry Division and the 303rd Medical Battalion received high command orders to cross the Ludendorff Bridge. At the west side of the bridge we waited momentarily to anticipate problems that might be encountered while crossing.

Army Movement to the Rhine River

It happened that we did encounter some unanticipated hazards that were immensely nerve-wracking. This bridge had been a railroad bridge and the railroad tracks and ties were scattered along the length of the bridge. Our military vehicles had to cross the bridge with this immense railroad devastation under our wheels.

Despite these risks, the 78th Infantry regiments and the 303rd Medical Battalion began crossing the significantly damaged railroad bridge. Our tanks, ambulances and other motorized vehicles had to carefully maneuver over displaced and broken railroad ties and tracks. During this trek, the bridge continued to sway and tremble very precariously.

My assignment was to remain in the rear of the Army truck, which was covered by a tarpaulin to protect Co. B medical and personnel records. While crossing the bridge, I observed with nervousness that several German planes were strafing and bombing the bridge. The record boxes were violently falling all over the place and becoming disorganized, due to the movement of the bridge. The truck was being driven by Sergeant Handsman with the Company Commander seated next to him. Although alone in the rear of the truck, I received very comforting verbal reassurance from Captain Linhart regarding the hazardous crossing.

As I tried to protect myself from the barrage, I did not have a feeling of fright or end of life. At one point, I even got curious enough to lift the tarpaulin to get an accurate view of the bridge and Rhine river. As I lifted the covering, I saw the overwhelming river below and its grand length and width, along with the bridge beams shifting back and forth. My calm feeling surprised me. There was absolutely no feeling of panic or sorrow.

Captain Randolph Linhart

Army Movement to the Rhine River

I began to speak to God and I thanked him for my wonderful life that he had given me, and I expressed my optimism that I would now join him in his heavenly paradise. This was my third encounter with possible death and the third time I realized that someone up there was watching over me and protecting me for some unknown reason.

The falling boxes and my curiosity distracted me periodically from the destruction going on around me. I heard the sound of two German Messerschmitt fighter planes flying over the Rhine River toward the bridge; both were firing at our vehicles and also attempting to drop bombs on the structure to cause its complete collapse. They were obviously hoping for Army units to fall into the river in a complete state of destruction.

Suddenly, I noticed about three or four American planes giving battle to the German aircraft. Given that they were greatly outnumbered, the German planes disappeared and did not have the opportunity to release their bombs.

There was armed infantry resistance from the enemy, but this minor rifle fire did not prevent the ultimate bridge crossing on March 7, 1945.

I will never forget the sight of the American Air Force at this vital period in time. Now, over 70 years later, this Ludendorff (Remagen) bridge encounter is still one of my most vivid memories of WWII.

After the armored units and infantry troops had successfully crossed and captured the Ludendorff Bridge, other U.S. divisions with engineering units had erected several pontoon bridges across the Rhine River. This occurred in anticipation of the collapse of the Ludendorff Bridge. The bridge finally collapsed on March 17, after the 78th Division, including my Company B, 303rd Medical Battalion, were entirely on the east side of the Rhine River and ready to advance further into Germany and towards Berlin.

Army Movement to the Rhine River

The German High Command, under Hitler's orders, held a German officer, Major Hans Scheller, responsible for not causing the complete destruction of the bridge before the arrival of the American troops. Although, some explosives were in place for timely detonation, the German High Command did not accept this and would not permit Major Scheller to go on without military punishment. He was executed by a firing squad in a wooded area about 30 miles east of the Rhine River.

Ludendorff Bridge on March 17, 1945

Shortly after the American troops had crossed the bridge, they were ready to move rapidly along the east bank of the Rhine River to occupy large German cities such as, Cologne (Koln), Wuppertal, Frankfurt, and Berlin.

At the east end of the bridge there was a railroad tunnel through a mountain and all the vehicles of our medical battalion were directed into this tunnel until the infantry regiments had checked the surrounding area for German troops and armaments.

After about two hours, the surrounding area was considered safe and our medical vehicles moved out, proceeding down the river road for about two miles to a large two-story building. There, we established our medical and surgical teams and set up our equipment. The time it took to get from the railroad bridge to the medical setup was approximately five hours. We remained at this location for about one week to provide medical help and supplies.

Army Movement to the Rhine River

A few hours after we arrived, I had the opportunity to go to the second floor of the building that we had established as our temporary 78th Division medical and surgical unit. As I looked out the window toward the Remagen bridge, I saw it totally collapse into the river, plunging many American soldiers and engineers to their deaths.

As mentioned before, the Army Engineers had worked quickly and diligently to build a pontoon bridge across the Rhine River strong enough to safely support troops, armored vehicles and armaments moving to the east side of the river. Within the next day or two they had safely erected about six similar bridges and the German forces were beginning full retreat. In 1988, the local German citizens in the town of Remagen and the U.S. Army erected a stone memorial near the bridge, recognizing the achievement of the 78th Infantry Division and all of its regiments and battalions. The 303rd

Medical Battalion is recognized on this memorial.

The Remagen bridge was never replaced, but the railroad tunnel entrance on the east side is still standing. Considering the abundance of brave men who risked their lives in the area, it is both nostalgic and warming to know that there are many present-day excursions, such as cruises going down the Rhine River, that now recognize this historic place as one of the main highlights of their cruise.

The next morning, the Division Chaplain came to our temporary location and celebrated Sunday morning Mass. It was at this Mass that I thanked God for my safe passage over the bridge; and from that date in 1945, I became a devoted religious being and have remained one to the present date.

The following day, we left our Rhine River medical location and proceeded north toward the large German cities of Koln (Cologne) and Wuppertal (a large industrial city). As we proceeded north, we passed the ruins of the Remagen (Ludendorff) bridge. My army vehicle drove by slowly and I once again wondered what could have resulted if my unit and myself were on the bridge at the time of the collapse; what if the German planes were not driven away by the U. S. Air Force and if they had successfully sprayed our vehicles with their heavy machine gun fire or had successfully completed the bombing of the bridge. Our company commander sent word to Co. B personnel that over 130 Army Engineers, who were working on the bridge specifically to reinforce it and prevent collapse, were killed or severely injured when it completely collapsed. Some drowned in the frigid river; others were violently struck by falling beams and other bridge structures. Our hearts were heavy as we prayed for these brave, selfless victims. All these thoughts are immensely clear in my mind, even today as a senior citizen, and they will remain equally as vivid throughout the remainder of my life.

General Dwight Eisenhower, commander of the American forces in Europe, stated to the world that, in his opinion, the successful capture of the Remagen bridge shortened the European war by six months and saved thousands of American and British lives. Many war experts agreed with him.

As we advanced along the east side of the Rhine River, we proceeded along a German super-highway named *Rheinischer Sagenweg*, which was my introduction to what we now refer to as a *freeway* or *thruway*. Please remember that the German road system in 1945 was far more advanced than the road system that I was familiar with in the Unites States.

The roads in the United States began to catch up to the remarkable German highways a decade later, in the mid 50's. The Germans initially built such a vast road system to assure that the German war machines could move more efficiently as they conquered and occupied neighboring European nations.

Army Movement to the Rhine River

Our first overnight stop since leaving Remagen was in the town Bad Honnef, a picturesque small city, with a beautiful view of the Rhine River. The structure of the home that we occupied for the one evening was also far more advanced in comparison to the home designs present in the United States. This home design started appearing in the United States much later, initially around the 1960s.

I noticed the modern kitchen, front entrance, living room, dining room and large second floor deck. This *typical* German home in this small town, made a lasting impression on me.

The following morning, we continued north along the German "freeway" until we reached the large and populous city of Koln (Cologne). We passed through but did not stop here because the city had already been occupied by other American and British troops. Over an extended period of time, this city took quite a beating from the American bombing raids. As I drove by in my vehicle, I observed the ruins and immense devastation. It was an unforgettable sight. A sight like this made me realize, once again, that this was *war.* It was both difficult and moving to see Koln (Cologne) in this state and to even potentially consider a city back home under similar ruin.

Remarkably, the only structure standing intact and with minimal damage was the Koln Cathedral. It stood like a monument to the sky, with miles of rubble surrounding it. I felt the immense symbolism behind this. Even earlier in the war, when the Germans bombed London and caused a wide range of destruction to residential, historical and governmental buildings, St. Paul's Cathedral was miraculously spared with little to no damage.

As we drove through Koln (Cologne), I continued to spend hours reflecting upon the power of God, due to witnessing him spare these magnificent structures. My previous dangerous experiences and the sight of the Koln miracle definitely affected my religious beliefs in a positive manner, not only then, but throughout my entire life.

After a few hours in the Koln (Cologne) area, Co. B accompanied the 78th Infantry Regiments eastward toward Berlin. The route took us through other heavily destroyed German cities, such as Wuppertal. Before the destruction done by American and British air might, Wuppertal was an iron and steel industrial city (like

Army Movement to the Rhine River

Pittsburgh, PA). Another German city that we passed was Kassel, which was equally destroyed. Smaller towns or bergs were also damaged and hit by war, but not nearly to the same extent.

12. Final Conflict Medical Set-Up

Our next extended medical set-up town was Beberbeck. This small berg is especially distinct in my memory. We established our medical unit for several weeks here, in a *horse-breeding farm*. It consisted of horses, horse stalls, exercise areas and unforgettable *horse manure pits*. You can be certain that the *aroma* on warmer days was quite overwhelming.

Very soon after we were medically established, we were visited by a kind woman, who lived in a small farmhouse a few hundred yards down the road. She offered to do laundry for those requesting the work. I did not even remotely hesitate; I immediately packed my dirty clothes in a bag and took them for a *well-needed* washing and ironing.

At her home, I noticed several small basement windows, like those back home. I recalled that at home, coal for the furnace was poured through the window and stored in the basement. At first glance, I assumed that coal was also stored in her basement, but instead, I discovered to my amazement that it was used to store potatoes. The entire basement room (size about 12x15 ft.) was filled.

Upon inquiry, I learned that potatoes were far more important than coal due to the lack of food; a direct result of the massive land destruction and contamination during the war. Potatoes were stubborn in the sense that they survived most of the damaged areas and were therefore stored and protected by the local residents. The food shortage became apparent during our stay in Beberbeck when we realized how desperately hungry the villagers were.

Our company kitchen was set up in the outside area near the barns. We would follow the food line with our mess kits and cups, which were filled with good quality meat, vegetables and coffee. When we finished eating, we deposited the remains in a large, metal garbage can. The leftovers for the entire company filled the can very generously.

I noticed a gathering of the villagers after the kitchen had closed and the G.I.'s had deposited the leftovers into the large cans. They reminded me of flies sinking into honey, hungry to the point that they were simply unable to resist (food from the *garbage*). The villagers came prepared with their pots and pans, and they proceeded to scoop up as much food as they could. This was the best food that they could find, but I must admit that it was rather sickening to watch.

This is what *war* can do to human dignity.

Never did any food scraps remain in the disposable cans after the villagers got to them. The thankfulness of the local population to be able to salvage these food scraps was unbelievable, beyond any comparison of words.

Our days in Beberbeck were quiet and uneventful as the war was rapidly coming to a conclusion. We treated some 78th Division soldiers, but primarily for minor illnesses and injuries.

As the days passed, I noticed and heard a conversation in the command post between Sergeant Robert Strusa (my unknown neighbor from back home) and First Sergeant Handsman, who I answered to, as the company clerk. I overheard Sergeant Handsman being referred to by the nickname, *Hank*, and I mistakenly thought that I could call him by this informal name.

He glared at me intensely as though he were breaking me with his eyes. He strongly stated that I had to refer to him as Sergeant Handsman.

He punished me by placing me on guard duty from midnight until 3:00 a.m. This meant that I had to patrol the entire perimeter of the horse farm compound for three whole hours in the dark of the night. The worst part is that I had to do this under minimal protection. I was given a simple stick, about the size of a small baseball bat, and that was to be my *weapon*, if needed.

Sergeant Handsman warned me that wild boars lived in the fields beyond the farm fences on the far side of the farm. I was told to stay alert, as these boars were often seen jumping the farm perimeter fence and were attracted to the manure pits.

During that three-hour assignment, I was a nervous wreck, especially when considering that I only had one stick to defend myself against boars and the darkness of the night. I intensely imagined boar sounds in the fields and in my head my three-hour shift turned into an eight-hour shift. It was a living nightmare.

When my shift eventually came to an end and my replacement arrived, I warned him about the boar danger. He immediately began to laugh heartily and said that he was told that this was a "set-up" and he only told me this because I was the company clerk who assigned duties such as this one and other needed assignments (such as kitchen police) to others.

The next morning, everyone in the command post had a hearty laugh. This practical joke on me may have provided fun and laughter for the company, but I can still visualize the darkness, the manure odors, the imaginary noises that I heard, and the stick that was my only defense.

Germany surrendered when the allied armies surrounded the capital city of Berlin, on May 5, 1945. The 78th Division and the 303rd Medical Battalion remained in the Beberbeck area (near Berlin) and provided medical service, but no longer for battle wounds.

13. Hospitalization in Frankfurt

As the days moved on, the weather warmed and improved with maximum sunshine; therefore, the company food and kitchen staff decided to set up serving tables in the courtyard. All the Co. B veterans brought their mess kits and cups outside (where they were served), and then sat down on a bench or on the grass in the courtyard and enjoyed their dinners.

Unfortunately, there was a bacterial enemy lingering about, due to the excessive amount of manure surrounding the yard. The wind blew the manure-based bacteria throughout the yard and infected some of the mess kit food. Five men and I were infected. A few hours after our meal, I was victimized with a severe stomachache that was strong enough to double me over and make it impossible for me and the others to walk.

Upon examination by our company commander, Captain Randolph Linhart, the diagnosis was acute hepatitis A. This form of hepatitis was directly a result of contaminated food and the only form of the disease known at the time. Now in the present day, medical science has discovered hepatitis B, caused by infected blood or bodily fluids, and hepatitis C, transmitted with infected blood by transfusion or illegal drug use. The fortunate side of my hepatitis attack was that it was not B or C type, which as I just mentioned, medical researchers had not yet identified in 1945.

The five other victims and I were transported by our company ambulances to a field hospital. Immediately upon arrival, a nurse insisted that I drink a liter of grape juice loaded with a full pound of diluted sugar. This drink contained so much sugar that as I drank it my lips became extremely sticky. The overwhelming sweetness was so powerful that I complained to the nurse that I could not drink it.

She insisted, raised the container to my mouth and observed as I gulped down the whole liter. She promised me that this would relieve my intense stomach pain.

Within one hour, she was proven correct, but the yellow tints on my skin and eyeballs remained. It was explained that hepatitis affects the liver and the liver bile was released in yellow color throughout my body. The doctor at the field hospital explained that all the victims were going to be transferred within the next two days to a large permanent hospital in Frankfurt, Germany, where several weeks of rest, special diets and proper medication would be given.

Before leaving for Frankfurt, our division commander, General Parker, made a visit to the field hospital. After a long while of visiting other hospitalized members of the 78th Division, he finally approached my bedside and immediately noticed my obvious yellow skin and eye condition. When the medical doctor explained to him that it was an infectious liver condition, he saluted me, wished me good health and then immediately left the hospital area. I believe that I appeared more frightening than movie monsters.

Upon arrival in Frankfurt, all the hospital's victims were given private rooms and underwent complete physical examinations. The rooms had comfortable beds, with much missed clean, pearly-white, sheets. A radio was also included; TV was not, because it was not available until several years later.

After three weeks in the hospital, the other victims had completely recovered and were discharged and transported back to Co. B, which had by then moved into the Berlin area. Unfortunately, my case was more severe, and I was not allowed to return to my unit at this time.

Although I had not completely recovered, my diet was no longer restricted, and I was finally allowed to eat anything that I had desired, including my favorite chocolate and vanilla ice cream. This was a real treat because at the time I had not tasted ice cream since we entered

Hospitalization in Frankfurt

the Battle of the Bulge in December 1944. Another nice advantage that I had received was more private attention from the U.S. Army nurses.

After a five week stay in Frankfurt, I was finally discharged and put on a train to Berlin, with my army equipment stored in a foot-locker. The train ride was three hours long, uneventful and spent in complete boredom. I left the train at my pick-up site in Berlin, where I was to wait for my next ride.

While waiting, two German boys, about 10-12 years of age, approached me and asked if they could carry my foot-locker to my billet. I explained that a Jeep was coming to pick me up, but I offered them a cigarette pack for their father as they requested, and a candy bar for each of them.

When my driver arrived, I received a strong lecture for giving them *too much*. I was amazed at this but had no regrets because I saw the smile on those kids' faces.

Germany had surrendered and the 78th Division, including Co. B of the 303rd Medical Battalion, were now stationed in West Berlin as an occupational division. Our medical unit continued to provide medical and health assistance to all the groups attached to the 78th Division, especially the 310th Infantry Regiment. Our medical unit was also available to give assistance to Berlin residents, if required. The near complete destruction of the city made it necessary to be on call to aid the residents. Many of those residents were deprived of food, clothing, medications and other basic home comforts.

Being in Berlin, seeing and living in the ugly aftermath of the war, I spent my spare hours reflecting upon the overall value and effect of a world at war. My thoughts brought me back to the killing of my company commander, Captain Andrew Heath, and the others in my unit that gave their lives for their country and for a better world. I could not visualize that from 1945 to 2018 there would be several more periods of death and destruction, that would *still* prove fruitless and continue mankind's unexplainable urge to destroy their own species.

Years after my honorable discharge, I received the opportunity of visiting military cemeteries in Belgium, Italy, France, and at Pearl

Hospitalization in Frankfurt

Harbor. I even paid an unforgettable visit to our nation's capital to see the Tomb of the Unknown Soldier and to observe the Arlington Cemetery, which is the final resting place of over 400,000 military personnel. The cemetery is pervaded with thousands of white crosses; it really makes military survivors such as myself wonder whether the efforts of these military men provoke a sense of gratitude among today's youth and whether people still have it in their hearts to care to keep making our country a better place.

As the after-war days rolled by, my thoughts began to turn to the idea of when I would be heading home. A point system was used as a fair way of honorably discharging veterans. Points were allocated based on the length of service. Those that entered military service on December 7, 1941 (Pearl Harbor Day), the day that the United States declared war, had a much greater number of points than vets such as me, who were inducted in 1943 or later. Sergeant Robert Strusa, my hometown friend, was inducted prior to Pearl Harbor Day and therefore had a maximum point total. He left for home several months before me and many others.

14. Furlough to Switzerland

While I awaited my point total to be enough to return to the USA, I continued my duties as company clerk. During this period, I had the opportunity to explore more of Berlin.

Fortunately, my company commander, Captain Randolph Linhart, granted me a furlough to Switzerland, which remains a remarkable experience and memory to this day. This furlough was taken in September 1945 and I was accompanied by a fellow Co. B medic. We were bused to Frankfurt, Germany, and then boarded a train to Basel, Switzerland. Basel is referred to as the "gateway to Switzerland." It is located on the Rhine River, near an immensely large railroad center.

From there we were transported by bus to Bern, the capital of Switzerland. Bern is located on the Aare River and is noted for its extraordinary medieval clock tower that regularly resounds with breathtaking chimes. After a day of sightseeing in Bern, we continued on to Geneva, the second largest city in Switzerland. Over the years, it has become known as the center of international diplomacy and is presently the home of several diplomatic organizations, such as the European headquarters of the United Nations and the International Red Cross. Geneva is one of the several picturesque cities located on Lake Geneva.

We continued our tour to Lausanne and Vevey. I spent several days here, admiring these lake resorts. My favorite part was witnessing dozens of small fishing boats decorating the beautiful, clear blue lake. The cities were both noticeably *clean*, filled with vibrant parks and highly decorated residential buildings. Almost every balcony that I saw was framed in a lovely manner by colorful flower arrangements. The majestic, snow-capped, towering Swiss Alps were mesmerizing to encounter in the background. They framed the cities in such a subtle, yet grand way.

The next part of our visit was Lucerne, which was noted for its two covered bridges; one of which had historical paintings on the inside walls. I spent several hours on the bridges, admiring the peaceful water views and the surreal talent behind the paintings. I came across a Swiss gentleman on one of the bridges, and he strongly suggested that I visit the famous "Lion of Lucerne;" a lion carved in solid rock on the side of the mountains, a magnificent memorial to the Swiss Guards. I decided to take his advice.

There was a well-known fable that stated that if you put your hand in the lion's open mouth, it would be bitten off. After a bit of hesitation and deliberation, I overcame a bit of anxiety and put my hand in the mouth of the lion. My nervousness must have been immensely apparent, because when I removed my shaking hand, not only was it still attached to my hand, but I was also applauded by a booming sound of laughter behind me. The surrounding citizens, while laughing, congratulated me and shook my (still shaking) hand.

Before leaving Lucerne, I had the opportunity to ride on a mountain train to the top of one of the nearby snow-capped mountains. I was immensely surprised to see the numerous village cabins and farmers herding and feeding their cows along the green mountainside. For a naïve G.I. from a rather limited and predictable neighborhood back in the United States, this city was probably the highlight of my Switzerland furlough. I was simply in another world.

Before departing this beautiful nation, I had the privilege of visiting its largest city, Zurich. Located on Lake Zurich, this city is noted for its beautiful and lush botanical gardens. It is also a large manufacturing and banking center, as well as a widely recognized center for learning. I especially enjoyed sight-seeing on foot through the vast shopping areas. During this, my thoughts would turn to back home; I recognized the massive gap in the financial and economic conditions when I compared Zurich to my hometown.

I had the pleasure of meeting a sweet, young Swiss girl, who joined me in window-shopping and then later walked with me to a lovely park on one of the city's many hills. I once again, admired the cleanliness and plethora of flowers that decorated my surroundings. After several hours of unexpected companionship, while I listened to her explain the history and the construction of this magnificent park, she had to leave for home. Her outside hours were restricted by her parents, due to the war conditions in Europe. She spoke English and I had the opportunity to thank her by giving her a goodbye hug and kiss. She was an unforgettable, kind-hearted and mature young lady who forever inhabits my fond memories.

Our Swiss furlough ended the next day and we left Zurich by train to Berlin to rejoin our medical battalion.

When we arrived back in the Berlin area, we learned that about fifteen enlisted men of our original Co. B Medical Battalion had been transferred to another division, which was scheduled to return to the United States to be honorably discharged from the United States Army. As mentioned before, this was based on the number of years and months served in combat and overseas areas. My close friend and fellow medic, Sergeant Robert Strusa was officially on the list and was homeward bound. In the meantime, new recruits had replaced those that had left, and I, as company clerk, was kept extremely busy, constantly updating the company records to include all the new assignments.

It was now mid-October, 1945, meaning it had already been five months since the war ended. The Berlin area was quiet and peaceful, and reconstruction of the heavily damaged city was underway. The German citizens became especially friendly and accepting of the American military as friends and neighbors. Many of them realized that some of their relatives were living in eastern Berlin, which was controlled by the Russian military. Economic conditions, including food and housing, were extremely poor here due to the Russian domination of government in their sector. Many tried to escape to western Berlin, which was under American control. To bring this possibility to a halt, the Russians built a sturdy, concrete and steel wall, to *permanently* divide the German capital. Several brave souls tried to cross the towering wall and were shot during their attempts at escape. A few people were lucky and successful, and I can imagine they felt that their lives were restored.

While this terrible restriction was ongoing, our medical unit had an abundance of quiet days, aside from giving standard medical attention to the military and the German citizens. The other members of Co. B and I had plenty of opportunities to do a fair amount of sightseeing in Berlin. Much of the city was still devastated, but the wondrous essence of the many historical sites remained priceless, despite that fact.

A few nightclubs had opened and were an outlet for the troops' newly acquired leisure time. I wanted to take full advantage of the leisure activities before me. I spent as much time as I could spare visiting the most renown areas of the city and enjoying an occasional glass of cold German beer. Please remember that at this point in my life, I was not much of a drinker.

A young, German *fräulein* that lived in the area befriended me, with her goal of marrying a U.S. serviceman in mind. With the completion of this goal, she would be eligible to immigrate to the United States with her *American husband*. She attempted to prove her *love* for me with hugs, kisses and tears; but to no avail, because I was still naïve and homesick enough to reject her attempts.

Within the next few days, an updated discharge point notice arrived, and I, with a total of 81 points, was included for the return to America. On November 25, 1945, I was transferred from the 78th Division, 303rd Medical Battalion in the Berlin district, to the 84th Infantry Division located in the Alsace-Lorraine region of Germany near the Belgian border. The 84th Division was moved to Camp Lucky Strike in this area, while the 78th Division remained in Berlin, where it was designated for occupation duty for the undetermined future. My assignment to the 84th Division at Camp Lucky Strike only lasted for three days. After that, we were transported by railroad to Le Havre, France, a major seaport on the English Channel.

Furlough to Switzerland

However, during our very short stay at Camp Lucky Strike, I had the great opportunity of visiting a grand concert hall nearby. This music building was erected before the 1900s and impressed me with its magnificent and complex architecture. A Germany symphony orchestra performed during my visit, honoring the classical music of famous composers. Up until this concert, I never truly expressed an appreciation for this type of music. Ever since, I have remained completely mesmerized by the talent of Beethoven, Chopin, Rachmaninov, Tchaikovsky, Bach, Mozart and several others. The concluding performance was "An der schönen blauen Donau," Opus 314 (known to us as the Blue Danube Waltz) by Johann Strauss II, composed in 1866. It is obvious that I am still absolutely impressed by this style of music, considering that I presently have an entire collection of it in my home.

15. Sailing Home

I would have returned the next day for another concert, but we boarded the train the next day for Le Havre, France. The railroad trip to Le Havre was relatively short and uneventful. We were billeted in army barracks overnight and then boarded our *Victory ship* to take us home.

Victory ships were mass-produced by the Kaiser Motor Co. during WWII, specifically for transporting troops, tanks, ammunition, munitions, food and medical supplies, all of which were required to win the war against Germany. They were smaller than most ocean vessels, but were neat and comfortable.

As soon as my fellow veterans and I were boarded, a general announcement was made, asking all personnel aboard who were attached to a medical unit to report to the ship's bridge. This included me, so I reported as told.

To my surprise, I was the only returning veteran aboard that had been assigned to a medical group. I explained to the officers in charge that my medical experience mostly consisted of clerical work, involving medical records and personnel records; I had no experience regarding blood work, injections, broken bones or caring for wounds of any sort.

Since I was the only medic veteran available, I was assigned to the sick bay to give medical attention to an Army Colonel that was recovering from a fatal noninfectious disease. His medical condition wasn't exactly horrible, it was rather good for the disease in question, but regardless, he had to remain in his sick bed for the entire trip home. My responsibilities were to take his temperature and pulse four times a day, and to make trips to the ships galley, to select and prepare the proper food for his very strict diet.

Due to my seasick experience on the way to Germany, in October 1944, I suspected that I might have a similar experience on the way back home. I had an immensely comfortable bed with a feathery, soft mattress and clean, pearly-white sheets. I was also able to use the fresh-water shower in the sick bay and had the privilege to select any food or dessert that appealed to me. I explained the seasickness possibility, but it fell on deaf ears and I had no choice but to take the assignment.

The next morning, the ship departed and it was only a few miles away from Le Havre when my worst fears came true. Keep in mind that in 1945 there were no medications or shots available for aiding seasickness as there are today. Ship stabilizers were poor and could not help in keeping the ship smoothly afloat. The only time that seasickness did not have a disastrous effect on me was when I laid flat on my back in my comfortable bed. I tried to spend as much time as possible in this position. I would get up periodically to take the Colonel's temperature and pulse, and then I would immediately rush back to my bed. I had to perfectly get the timing down to avoid vomiting. My trips to the galley to get food had to be timed with additional caution. With luck, good planning and timing, I managed to successfully complete these tasks and immediately make it back to either my room or the toilet to vomit. With more experience and knowing what to expect, the trip back home seemed a bit faster than the trip to Europe.

I had full access to all the food available, but as my stomach was sensitive, my diet was severely limited. My desire for (hard to find) ice cream was a casualty and it was an unbelievable struggle for me to avoid all the ice cream before me. I thought about ice cream during my entire voyage home. In addition, I had to give up my privilege of taking hot, fresh-water showers, because I could not remain on my feet long enough to avoid throwing up.

With my handicaps, as just explained, I ultimately managed to complete my medical assignments, which was the important part; but

Sailing Home

I must say that it was a shame that I could not take full advantage of all the luxurious privileges that I had in front of me.

After a few days of frequent seasickness, I was confronted one morning by three high-ranking officers, who came to visit the Colonel. They found him in good spirits and even though he complimented my regular assistance, one of the officers noticed that I was prone in bed during their visit. My explanation for this was not sufficient and he called me a "goldbrick" (a soldier who avoids assigned duties). He threatened to charge me for not performing my assignment. One of the other officers explained to him that I had carried out my duties in spite of my seasick condition. Apparently, the officer who defended me was familiar with seasickness through his own personal experience.

When our Victory ship was approximately 24 hours from our New York port, I miraculously recovered and as soon as I became aware, I went to the freshwater shower to enjoy something that seemed to me a gift for good conduct. I also did not hesitate to eat a large volume of ice cream to celebrate. To this day, ice cream is still my favorite dessert and it was never available to me in the Army, except in the hospital in Frankfurt.

As we approached New York City, the skyline glowed, radiantly welcoming us. New York fire boats were patiently waiting in the harbor and as we passed the Statue of Liberty, they all turned on their fire hoses, shooting strong water streams into the air all around the Victory ships, bringing us home. This was a tribute in our honor and a thank you for faithful service. It was completely unexpected. As we saluted the fire boats and the flags of the United States, a few tears rolled down my cheek, as I tried to explain to myself the reality of New York City preparing such a grand honor for returning veterans.

Almost immediately upon dock arrival, we disembarked and boarded Army buses, while many spectators loudly applauded, and an Army band played the National Anthem and "God Bless America." Even to this day, I am still extremely impressed by this tribute.

16. Honorable Discharge

After the short amount of time that was allowed for us to appreciate this unexpected honor, we departed in buses for the short journey to Fort Dix, New Jersey. After arrival, a rather lengthy discharge procedure commenced; which included a complete physical exam, a review of our inoculations, mental and psychological debriefing and encouragement to take advantage of all opportunities provided for honorably discharged veterans in the G.I. Bill of Rights.

After these necessary procedures were completed, we were assigned to a cot and sleeping area. We were told that in the morning we would receive our railroad tickets for our personal destinations.

When dawn arrived, we were awoken at an early hour, as expected. This is always traditional in the service. We then had breakfast, gathered our belongings, received our transportation tickets, $60 discharge pay and our honorable discharge documents. Then we were told to board a bus that would take us to the railroad station.

My bus took me to Trenton, New Jersey, to wait for the Pennsylvania railroad train that would take me to Buffalo. Apparently, I was the only G.I. going in that direction, therefore, I was left all alone on the railroad platform, as I waited for my train to arrive.

After an hour-long wait, my train had arrived. I boarded, found a comfortable coach seat and prepared myself for a slow and uneventful trip home. While on the train, I had the time and opportunity to recall and reflect upon my total military experience, from the time that I entered the guarded gates at Fort Niagara, on January 23, 1943, to my discharge date of January 26, 1946.

Now that I have completed this phase of my life, what else would the future have in store for me? At this point, I had absolutely no clue, except that I definitely knew that I wanted to get a college degree. This was made possible for me under the G.I. Bill.

As the train moved through Western New York, more familiar sights appeared in the countryside. Soon enough, we were cruising through the Buffalo suburbs. Finally, the train arrived in the downtown railroad station.

As soon as I de-boarded, I saw my mother and father running toward me, with their arms wide open. My parents hugged and embraced me with welcome home kisses and tears of pure happiness.

The military era of my life had ended. I had entered the service as an utterly naïve youth, but now I was ready to step into the void and begin the next unknown phase of my life. Even 70+ years later, the logical and compassionate experiences that I have encountered and endured, remain vivid and crucial to me.

December 21, 1944: the date that Captain Andrew Heath was killed by German 88 mm shelling. April 8, 1945: the date that the Ludendorff Bridge at Remagen could have collapsed while the Co. B Medical Battalion was crossing. These events will never be forgotten and will be remembered constantly by this writer. During church services and prayer, my mind always exclaims, "why me?" I feel strongly, with every fiber of my being, that someone up there was watching over me and is continuing to do so. As my life span is concluding, I wonder if I have successfully made my contribution to mankind as God has wanted.

Epilogue

My military career concluded on January 26, 1946, five days before my 23rd birthday. After two days at home accepting greetings and congratulations, I drove to Hayes Hall at the University of Buffalo to register for classes using the benefits awarded me by the GI Bill of Rights. My career ambition was to become a certified public accountant. I enrolled in the UB Business Management School and began my college education in February 1946. I was awarded 16 credits for my completion of the Princeton University ASTP engineering program. This allowed me to earn and receive my B.S. degree with an accounting major in January of 1948.

To receive my CPA certification, I was required to complete at least one year of accounting experience with a local accounting firm. I began my required year with a local Buffalo firm. As the weeks were spent doing menial tax and accounting work, I gradually realized that this was not my career goal. After very careful thought, I changed my career path to Public School Secondary School Education. I returned to the UB campus and registered with the School of Education. I received my teaching certification in January of 1949.

My first contact with teenage students was as a student teacher at Riverside High School in Buffalo. As my teaching time progressed, I became confident that this was my true career path. Teaching positions were very hard to find, and I sent my resume to every school district in Western New York. Fortunately, I was offered a

89

position as a business teacher at Alden Central School beginning in September of 1950.

Following four years of courtship which began on February 7, 1946, (soon after my discharge). I married my wife, Irene, on November 23, 1950, which happened to be Thanksgiving Day. We lived at 41 Pavonia Street located off Hertel Avenue near Military Road. Living there and teaching in Alden required long daily drives on pre-expressway country roads. It was difficult and tiring, but I was determined to keep this teaching position and continue my career in education.

After two years at Alden, I was happy to receive an offer from Superintendant James Green with the City of Tonawanda School System. In September of 1952, I began my 37 year-long teaching and administrative career at Tonawanda High School. I had an opportunity to teach each of the available business courses, including my favorite programs in Bookkeeping and Business Law.

In 1963, I was appointed Director of Continuing Education. This evening program was in session Monday through Thursday from 6 p.m. until 9:30 p.m. at the high school and it grew rapidly. It appealed to working adults and parents who had not previously had the opportunity to improve their personal education. My teaching and administration hours were long and tiresome on many occasions, but I received the handsome salary of $3200 for day school teaching and $100 for evening administration duties!

In April of 1952 my son, Paul, was born, and in March of 1955 my daughter, Susan, arrived. With two children who needed my time and attention, I had to cut back on my evening school duties, so I resigned as Director of Adult Education. In 1968, I was fortunate enough to be selected as program director of a new program called the T.H.S. Work Experience. This effort was aimed at students whose future was not expected to include a college education. My role was to contact local employers and describe the program and the advantages it could provide to students and employers. The program took me out of the classroom part of each day and put me out in the community contacting local businessmen. It was a very satisfying

Epilogue

experience and most of our students felt that they were part of a stimulating and useful educational program.

When the assistant high school principal retired in June of 1971, I was asked to apply for the position. Fortunately, I was chosen for the job and began a new phase of my career in education which continued to my retirement in 1989. This completed a stimulating and satisfying 39-year career in public school education.

Until his death in 1988, my family had a wonderful social relationship with former Staff Sergeant Strusa, his wife Rita and his children, Daniel and Barbara. Following his death, his grandson, Joseph Elliott, began extensive research on the military awards and medals earned by Sgt. Strusa, but never awarded during his lifetime. As part of his investigation, he became determined to petition military authorities to obtain my long overdue medals too. As a result, in July of 2014, Congressman Brian Higgins presented me with my awards, including a Bronze Star, during a ceremony at Kenney Field in the Town of Tonawanda.

While conducting his military research, Joseph Elliott learned about Captain Andrew Heath's daughter, Margaret, who was about two years of age when her father was killed. When Joseph contacted her and informed her of the circumstances which linked me to her father, she expressed her sorrow over the lost contributions to the field of medicine which his untimely death had caused. She knew nothing about me or my existence and she wondered why I had survived while her father had died. Fortunately, when she learned of my career accomplishments as a high school teacher and administrator, she contacted me to tell me that her heart was at rest knowing what I had accomplished during my life. To this day, we stay in contact via the internet.

Randy Linhart, Jr., son of Captain Linhart, my second company commander, and I are in regular contact by phone and visits to my home.

Time does not diminish my vivid recollections of the death and destruction that occurred during my war years, from January, 1943 until January, 1946. The clarity of the frightening, personal and group experiences remain in my heart and soul to this very day, over 70 years since the surrender and defeat of the German and Japanese war machines. Our victories were made ultimately possible by the dedication and determination of all the citizens in the United States who proudly supported their country until the successful conclusion of the war.

Men enlisted in the various branches of the military service, while women typically went to work for automobile and aircraft companies to produce tanks, planes and ammunition, or enlisted in the service as female military personnel and nurses. All their contributions were essential to our victory.

Our allies (including the United Kingdom, France, Canada, Australia, Norway, Sweden, Russia, China, India, Yugoslavia and many other countries), made essential contributions in the Atlantic and Pacific war zones. Without their aid, the final (successful) outcome may have been delayed or may not have occurred. In the years since WWII ended, our nation has continued in its determination to remain free and independent. It has continued to assure that our future generations, children and adults, would forever remember the ultimate sacrifices made by millions of servicemen, not only in WWII, but also in North Korea, Vietnam and the Middle East. Those brave souls, especially those that have been wounded or disabled, deserve to know that their sacrifices were not in vain.

They all deserve endless respect for their service.

It has been over seventy years since the war has ended, and considering the battles fought and the sacrifices made to assure victory for our citizens and our nation, I still feel the same pride for my service and my country. I am worried though, that such pride is becoming a distant memory for future generations. Both public and private school educators must continue to emphasize the sacrifices that all military personnel and civilian industrial workers made for our country. Perhaps I am assessing the future of our beloved nation in a rather pessimistic fashion, but I can't help but show concern for such a thing. Future generations should be encouraged and reminded about the sacrifices made by millions of United States veterans to successfully maintain our freedom-loving government.

Epilogue

I was recently selected to be included in an Honor Flight to visit the recently completed WWII memorial, the Korean and Vietnam memorials, the Iwo Jima monument and the Tomb of the Unknown Soldier. Instead of a direct bus ride to the Tomb, our bus driver took the "scenic route" and drove through the greater portion of Arlington Cemetery. As we proceeded, I saw an endless number of white crosses, facing various directions. The driver informed me that I was staring at over 400,000 military graves.

I hope my humble and patriotic contribution to the successful war effort has been appreciated by the citizens of our country. Those veterans resting under these crosses deserve the same appreciation and should forever be gratefully remembered.

GOD BLESS AMERICA!

INDEX

Index

ABOUT THE AUTHOR

From a press release issued by Congressman Brian Higgins on Jul 2, 2014:

"'Corporal Lawrence Titzler played a valuable role in ensuring the safety of his fellow infantrymen and the eventual Allied victory," said Congressman Higgins. "It is truly our honor to present him with this symbol of a nation's appreciation [a Bronze Star Medal]."

"Born in 1923, Mr. Titzler entered the United States Army on January 23rd, 1943 amidst the nation's involvement in World War II and bravely served his country in the Rhineland region during the European conflict. Mr. Titzler was studying engineering at Princeton University under the Army Specialized Training Program (ASTP) when he was transferred to the 303rd Medical Battalion, which was part of the 78th Infantry Division.

"After completed training, in November of 1944, Company B boarded the USS John Ericsson and eleven days later landed in Bournemouth, England. They crossed the English Channel landing in France, boarded a train, passed through Belgium and eventually into Germany. By December of 1944, the 303rd Medical Battalion was directly supporting the men of the 78th Infantry Division. As a member of Company B of the Army's 303rd Medical Battalion, Corporal Titzler served as a frontline medic in charge of processing troop information related to troop movement to prepare other medics for responding to injuries sustained on the front lines. CPL Titzler and the 303rd Medical Battalion went on to participate in some of the most historically significant battles in Germany including the "Battle at Remagen" and the "Battle of the Bulge."

"After May 8, 1945, Victory in Europe Day (VE Day), the 78th was sent to Berlin. CPL Titzler left Europe in January of 1946 and was honorably discharged a month later.

"Titzler returned home to complete his college education. He worked as a respected business teacher for 21 years, while raising his family with his wife Irene and eventually assumed the role of Assistant Principal at Tonawanda High School, a position he held for nearly 20 years."

Made in the USA
Columbia, SC
12 July 2018